a day in the life of...
100 women in Britain

EDITED BY ROSA MATHESON
ASSISTED BY HANNA-GAEL DARNEY

DESIGNED and SUB-EDITED BY KATE PARSONS
www.parsonscreative.co.uk

the BOOK PROJECT
www.the100womenbookproject.com

First published 2011

Published by
The Book Project
Highworth SN6 7PG
Wiltshire U.K.

British Library Cataloguing in Publication Data.
A catalogue record for this book is available from the British Library.

ISBN 978-0-9570471-0-5

Design, sub-editing, typesetting and origination by
Kate Parsons – www.parsonscreative.co.uk – Swindon, Wiltshire U.K.

Printed in U.K.

contents

I Love What I'm Doing

Woman in a Man's World

A Special Day

Not What I Expected

acknowledgements

One thing I have learned over my book-writing years is that putting a book together is truly a team effort. There are always people who need to be thanked and appreciated.

First and foremost I would like to thank all those women who took the time, made the effort and did the writing, without them we would not have a book. Secondly I would like to thank my family who urged on and encouraged their friends and colleagues to participate.

Undoubtedly a *very* special thanks is due to Kate Parsons who has designed and put this wonderfully attractive book together as her support of the project. Another goes to Amy Rigg, my editor at The History Press, who gave me the benefit of her experience and constantly suggested and advised.

Lastly, although this is a 'women's book', there are also men who deserve thanks namely Roger Ogle of Swindon Link Magazine who offered support and contacts that proved very fruitful; Rod Shaw who came up with a very helpful costing for the printing and advised and held my hand all the way through, Ian Drummond for always being at the end of the telephone with advice, and, as always, my husband Ian for his support of and enthusiasm for the project, and for me.

introduction

**Funny, feisty, tender and sad
are just some of the emotions
captured in the words of 100 women,
aged eighteen to ninety five,
which make up this most unusual
and fascinating book.**

**Given the opportunity to take part
in 'the Book Project' to help less
fortunate women on the
'other side of the world,'
100 women 'here' in Britain
took to their pens (or laptops) to
help women 'there' in Nepal.**

**Writing of daily routines, special
events and personal experiences,
they have created a human 'snapshot'
of women's lives in Britain in
the 21st Century.**

New beginnings

Jayne Workman

This is my professional name, married name Hughes.
Married, living in Ilkley, West Yorkshire.

New Places

Powdery snow. Pale sky. Glistening hills. The delicate blue of the morning rises behind the gentle curves of distant moortops glinting in the brave winter sun. Nearer, lines of untouched snow mark out feathery fronds of pine and the black-brown claws of bare trees. This is Yorkshire. It's cold. Very cold. And, it's nearly Christmas.

Sitting here in the warmth, my eyes stare, as if by staring I can keep it. At least, in my mind. The longer I look, the clearer it will stay. Because, this time next year I won't be here. We won't be here. We'll be on the other side of the world. Yes, we're leaving.

When we started this more than a year and a half ago, it was a dream, an exciting plan for the future. Now it's upon us, I see the world, my world, with different eyes. Everything is coloured by the knowledge that this could be our last – our last English winter, our last white Christmas, our last few months with family and friends. This is what change does. It makes you see what you have afresh. It fills your heart with a powerful blend of sentimentality, fear and, oh yes, a sense of drama. This move, though still far enough away to be distant, is close enough to make everything else feel temporary. I'm frightened of leaving behind what I know and enjoy. I'm frightened of making a mistake.

But this is nothing new. I've had new beginnings before. I should know by now the tricks the mind can play, its readiness to confuse, to distort, to confound. Clarity is often to be found in the gut, in the heart, in the vision seen from afar. It's in the thick of it, caught up in the detail, the smaller decisions, that it's easy to lose sight of the reason, the glittering prize, that brought you here in the first place; the promise of new experiences and a different life. What will it be like to live by the beach, to watch the whales, to surf, to ski, to soak in the hot springs? How will it feel to wake up every day in another country? There's excitement just in that.

There's uncertainty too, of course. We know. But how easy, in the middle of life, to sit back and enjoy the pleasures of living in one place; the warmth of lifelong friends, the closeness of family, of knowing, understanding and of feeling safe. So, I remind myself to reclaim a lightness of heart, a sense of adventure and the opportunity to play with life. Because we're lucky to have it.

Maybe one day, I'll stare out of a different window in a different place, one I don't know yet. And I'll feel the same mix of fear, excitement as I try to soak up every last drop of what's in front of me. For now, though, I have to take a leap of faith. For new beginnings, you have to.

----o-O-o----

Anna Hoffman

*28, born in Germany, living in England for the past five years.
I went to Nepal last year to teach English at Buddhist monasteries and
am delighted that I can contribute to another good deed.*

Making it Happen

Waking up this morning I'm thinking how lucky I am having a roof upon my head, plenty of food and clean water, to be able to enjoy a moderate life style and, most of all, to have a job I enjoy which provides for all these things.

I remember once being asked in an interview what had been my biggest achievement in life. I couldn't think of anything. It took me a few weeks to realise that my biggest achievement in fact had been to set up an existence in a foreign country all on my own. I'm actually proud to look back and see how far I have come. I clearly remember the day when I decided that I wanted to stay in England instead of going back to Germany where I was born and had spent the past twenty-three years.

I had terminated the work experience which had brought me here and, despite having had just about enough money for a return flight home and no prospect of work or a place to live, I still knew that I had to stay since for the first time in my life I had felt at home. Also, I remember that the day after I had quit the work experience I was already regretting my decision. It was Sunday and not a lot could be done about finding a job or a flat. Maybe I had been a bit too eager in my decision, I thought. However, by the end of the next day I had already found a room in a lovely house under miraculous circumstances. But I only had the money for the deposit and three weeks rent. I registered with all the major recruitment agencies in town and little by little the work would come in. A couple hours kitchen work and a few hours as a waitress, then a couple of days cleaning and few days data entry – I did almost everything – which in the end paid the rent for more than just three weeks.

At times I felt utterly lonely and wondered what it was that I was running away from. And it was also a bit daunting with all the legal aspects from opening a bank account, actually first of all finding a bank who would take me on, to receiving a national insurance number. But somehow there was always someone there to help me and I knew that whatever would happen was supposed to happen.

It did take three years until I had built a more or less stable circle of friends and another year to meet a truly lovely man. I had unsettling relationships which only made me stronger. I pursued new interests and took up old ones again. I met wonderful people who became friends and in the end I can even say that I am grateful to my bullying childhood teacher for not permitting me to attend French lessons but making me have extra English lessons instead.

In Germany I had initially trained in Graphic Design and then retrained as a Foreign Language Secretary because I had decided that I wanted to go abroad. Now, however, I am a Health Care Assistant at the local hospital and have gained a few qualifications on the job. And it turns out to be the only job so far that gives me the truly rewarding feeling of doing something that matters and makes a difference.

I wonder if all of this would have happened if I had stayed in Germany. I will never know for sure, but I do know that I wouldn't be the same person I am today. I am divinely grateful for having found my way over here knowing that I have made a difference not only to my own but to also to the lives of many other people that I have met and cared for during the last years. I look out of the window, thinking, what a gorgeous new day. What shall I do now?

Diane Sleigh

43, bee keeper and vegetable grower. Live in a house on a farm near Westbury, Wiltshire. Moved here from London where I had been living and working for twenty three years. Single

Moving Home

Like so many people these days, I'm a new beekeeper. I'd seen a demonstration at the Royal Show in 2008 which inspired me to attend a taster day at a city farm in north London where I lived. The touch paper was lit. But I lived in London, how was I going to keep a beehive (with at least 50,000 bees in the summer) in my small urban garden whilst still being able to use it myself? Hmm, maybe the beekeeping would just have to wait.

I was working as an IT Project Manager in the City of London for an international broking firm and had worked in London doing various jobs since I was eighteen (some time ago).

I'm originally from Worcestershire, fairly rural but not farming. Every year or so since I was about thirty-five years old I thought about moving out of London, back to the country but what to do when I got there?

Well, what about the bees? I sat in front of a careers advisor when I was at school with no idea what I wanted to do with my life. I've been fortunate, met some great people and had some interesting jobs but they were jobs, they didn't really raise a passion in me. But from the little idea of being able to keep bees and harvest honey grew my idea of growing vegetables, keep some hens, maybe even pigs some day, I just wanted enough to be sustainable and have a little over to barter or sell. Right, I liked that idea so when was I going to do it? How long did I want to keep on being an IT Project Manager? I was forty one years old. Five years? Two? Hmm, I don't think I want to be doing this by the end of the year (it was May). Ok then, let's start thinking and get going.

I moved to Wiltshire two years ago and am loving it. I got a part time job, a big change from working full time all my life and less money but I really enjoy it. I found my local beekeepers association, joined up and took a course. I've met some lovely people; generous, knowledgeable and willing to help with all sorts (and some oddballs too of course!).

I bought a hive, flat pack and put it together (who knew there were such things!) and with the help of my tutor, we installed my first colony of bees in their new hive in my garden in May 2009. Several times a day I sat in the grass reading my book near the hive, if you sit by the entrance on the side that they are not coming and going from, the girls go about their business of collecting nectar and pollen and have no interest in you at all. It's fascinating, their little pollen baskets bulging with pollen of all colours of the rainbow depending on which flowers are in season and being visited.

My first lovely hive, called No. 9 as that was their number when they came from my tutor, flourished and I gratefully received 20lbs of honey from them whilst leaving them plenty for their winter stores. They were soon joined by two more colonies that summer and as I look at the snow of winter 2010, I have nine colonies that are clustered inside their hives keeping each other warm.

Next year, I will try a few more veg.

------o-O-o------

Henrike von Werder

From Germany, studying an MA in History of Gardens at University of Bristol.

Studies in Foreign Parts

My name is Henrike, I am a twenty-five year old student from Germany, who just moved to Bristol to study 'Garden History' at University of Bristol. With today my 'new' life has started, far away from home, family and friends. Naturally it didn't turn 180 degree within twenty four hours and I had expected myself to wake up this morning recapitulating the last months. However, my thoughts were more like "Come on, what's that noise? Please, I wanna sleep!" My radio went on at 7am; I realized that there was some noise at 7:14; my alarm started to ring at 7:30, but I couldn't get out of bed until 7:40. Sounds familiar? Well, nothing has really changed on that part of my life!

Once I finally got up, I did what I do every morning here: I scuffled upstairs to the bathroom, got dressed and had breakfast. Quite unusually I caught the bus even before any of my housemates came downstairs. Typically for German punctuality I arrived at the Botanic Garden twenty eight minutes early, where we would meet our fellow students for the first time and would have a guided tour. I waited and waited and watched every person going in and coming out of the Botanic Garden carefully. For the first time in the last four weeks – since I had arrived in Great Britain – I was nervous. Eventually I felt relieved when a man showed up who looked just like my 'new' Professor I had seen on some pictures on the internet. The nervousness turned into excitement.

How had it all begun? It was in the beginning of the final year of my History of Art studies when the professor told us about an MA program, which is only offered at University of Bristol and which went so well with my interests: Garden History. It took one second to make the decision but hours, days, weeks and month to get along with bureaucracy, to organise moving out and in, to say goodbye, to choose what I would take, definitely not or maybe with me –

6

dependant on what accommodation I might find, to locate suitable rooms to let, to arrange viewings for those, to finally book a flight and a bed while all that time I was still writing my BA thesis. What made me make the decision to move to a county whose language I might speak fluently but far from being perfect? To move to a city where I know no one? To graduate eventually there? Pure interest and a strong confidence in achievement. I didn't care whether I knew anybody or not. I had been tired of my everyday life in Düsseldorf, Germany. I needed a change at least for a while.

However, when I joined the group of my fellow students I felt a bit disappointed. Due to my History of Art studies I am used to 'older' students and know that men are rare. So I wasn't surprised to find just one man between nineteen women. Nevertheless did I not expect myself to be the youngest. By far the youngest! All of them are married and have – mostly grown-up – children. So there I stood, single, still dependent on my parent's money. It still feels awkward! Yet it sounds more terrible than it actually is. That I realized very soon. After registration I went with the 'girls' for a coffee and though they are mostly my mother's age, they are really fun. We had a good laugh and I'm honestly looking forward to our trip to Oxfordshire. What's better than being amongst wiser women?

Anthea Beaumont

A former librarian, have worked at the Foreign Office library with the poet Fleur Adcock, as well as in public and academic libraries. I have always enjoyed writing, including several plays for my W.I. drama group, and last year won a competition to become Poet Laureate of Highworth (the prize was signed by the real Poet Laureate, Carol Ann Duffy!)

First Day

So…today is the first day of my new life, the day I am officially deemed to be too old to work, the day I formally slip into the 'third age', the first day of my retirement. Flown by are the last forty and more years of my life, the years of higher education, paid employment, marriage and babies, then more paid employment. Where did these years go?

Leaving aside the vexed question of housework, today is the first day of my life (yes, even as a child I was beholden to my parents' wishes) that I don't 'have' to do something if I don't want to do it. No more boring, frustrating journeys to a place of work in constant turmoil, where all too often creativity is stifled and management diktats smother enjoyment. No more battling for fundamental rights, or working out responses to yet another proposed restructuring.

There are challenges ahead. No-one likes getting older and women in particular far too often suffer the indignity of becoming the invisible 'little old lady', regarded by the young as a burden on the state. Then there is the challenge of being at home with one's husband twenty four hours a day. I am of a generation of women who, thanks to the feminist movement, step-by-step acquired an independence unknown by our mothers. How do I adapt to the routine of a husband who has already been retired for many years? Will he want to do everything with me when I have my own plans for how I want to spend the rest of my life? How will I put up with the mess he makes when my instinct is to clear up immediately? How, indeed, will we manage with one computer (let alone one kitchen, when he has done the cooking for the last sixteen years?)

So many things I want to do...and so little time. There are places and things I always wanted to see, from the mysteries of the Arctic and the Northern lights to the colours, music and tastes of the Spice Islands and the blue Caribbean, from remote Scottish islands to the marvels of the Antipodes. There are poems as yet unwritten, plays to publish, photographs to take, research to undertake, family history to explore. So many books to read, so much knowledge to acquire, here, now, quickly, before the eyes get too tired and the fingers too trembling. The grandchildren to cherish as they grow up before our eyes, the relatives and friends for whom I never had enough time, the elderly, sick and lonely members of my church and the wider community to help. Looking out of the window I see the weeds in the garden, the fallen leaves, the patches of bare earth crying out to be filled with the colour and foliage of new plants. Indoors there are cupboards to clear, papers to sort, old clothes to dispose of, dusty corners to clean.

Out of the chrysalis emerges a new woman, older but (I hope) wiser, ready for the new day.

Shirley Willis

Born 1949 in Borehamwood, Herts. Spent most of my working life involved with horses and ponies. Since retiring some four years ago, have devoted my life to travelling with my husband David in our motorhome throughout the UK and Europe. Am keen cyclist, like doing crosswords and, obviously, travelling.

Retirement

Some dread it, some won't take to it but we love it – *retirement*.

After both passing sixty, we decided on a complete life change. The window that exists between retirement and 'the wheelchair' has to be grabbed and time used to the full extent. Think about it, plan it, work it all out and then *do it*.

When the last of the children left for University we started our journey. We had three horses, four acres of paddocks and stables, the house was isolated, and the one acre of garden was great but didn't fit into our plans, so we sold the lot, lock stock and barrel. We found a house of similar size in the safety of a little village with a much more manageable garden. Here we plan our dreams of travelling in our 'Five star hotel on wheels' motorhome. We normally spend two to eight weeks away at a time either in Europe or our beautiful UK.

Having just returned from the west coast of Scotland, where we meandered slowly along quiet single track roads admiring the views of the hills or coast line, stopping or deviating as the mood took us. A typical day included wild parking, lochside, alone (apart from sheep) in a stunning glen with mountains all around. We would awake to magnificent views with the morning mist just lifting off the water. After morning tea and a hot shower, I walk the dog, Russ, whilst 'the other half' makes the bed and the breakfast. I take the binoculars and spot the odd eider duck or red-breasted merganser on the loch. During breakfast we plan our day. Having been told there are eagles nesting a few miles away, with the weather looking good we decide to set off on the bikes to our destination and sit and wait. Our time is not wasted when we are rewarded with a magnificent flying display from these wonderful creatures with eight foot wing span and capabilities of gliding on the wind for minutes at a time. Then a six mile cycle ride to the hotel for a possible snack and a newspaper.

We return to the motorhome and to be greeted by Russ, who has enjoyed his morning snooze. We read the paper and do the crossword, enjoy a puzzle, do a little model painting – whatever takes our fancy – even a little sun worshipping when available!

Russ reminds us a walk is needed so we set off down the loch to where it opens out towards the sea. We spot a few grey seals popping their heads up to see what we are up to – they are so nosy. We have the binoculars in the hope of spotting an otter or two, no luck just eiders and oyster catchers. Back to our cosy motorhome, if it has been bright the solar panel will have fully charged the leisure battery and we can watch a little television and watch the sun go down over the water with all its amazing colour changes and highlights. So to planning our next adventure and stopping place; maybe a boat trip to an island or into a town to learn its history – this often assisted by the ordnance survey maps borrowed from our local library, a very helpful source of free information. And so to bed.

As you can see our life is one long round of decisions. Come rain or shine it is always amazing, exciting and we love it.

Ioli Pieri

Mother of three, proud Nanny. Lives in Highworth.
Qualified hairdresser and trained counsellor.

A Rush of Love

The news although a surprise was met with great excitement, life changing for us all. We all began to accept, some with elation others more muted, but this was a decision made and wasn't going to change, I was going to be a grandmother!

Then reality stepped in. A routine hospital visit changed everything. There were major complications! Tears, lots of them, were shed by all, what were they going to do? A major choice to make, the feeling of helplessness I will never forget. The decision made, tests were done, and not all as expected, we were still left with uncertainty. Life is never as we expect it.

I was going to be a grandmother; I would have my very first grandchild how wonderful!

How was I going to do such an important job? A job that I had no experience of? I had no role model, no mother to tell. My mum died when I was expecting my eldest daughter, who is now expecting her own baby.

My family was growing, this is the next generation, I became the head of the family. I suppose I already was but hadn't really thought about it. What a responsibility. What was I going to do? I had heard of families falling apart because of interfering grandmothers, how would I get it right? How would my other children feel about having a baby in their family? Surprisingly they loved the thought of becoming an aunt and uncle.

I was extremely lucky and will always be immensely grateful to my daughter as I was included in all her preparations for the baby; thinking of it still makes me emotional and I hope it was as nice for her as for me. I was able to do for her what mum couldn't do for me. We went shopping for the baby; we discussed pros and cons of equipment although they made up their own mind in the end. I helped with visits to the hospital and because of the complications there were quite a few, some of those visits made us laugh, others filled us with frustration. I remember lots of tea drunk, but no coffee as it made her feel sick!

Eventually my not quite son-in-law called to say that they were on the way to the hospital as my daughter was in labour. This was it! Only a few hours and we would know.

It was the worst night of my life!

My youngest daughter was watching High School Musical 2 on DVD repeatedly. My son was concerned but oblivious. I was decorating the kitchen; I don't think I have ever decorated as late. Eventually at 3 am I went to bed, and lay just praying all would be well. 6am came and still no call, what had happened? Should I phone the hospital? Would that be acceptable? What had gone wrong? Was everything alright? I remember stood on that day by the kettle in the newly decorated kitchen that still needed cleaning making a cup of tea. This was going to be a very special day; one that would change my life. My world would never ever be the same. I had no idea just quite how that would be so true.

I spoke to the proud dad at 07:10 that morning, all was well, the baby was fine and healthy a beautiful baby boy, my daughter exhausted yet thrilled.

Later on that morning I was able to see them all. It was decided I would stay with mum and baby while dad went home to rest. My daughter fell asleep while I held my grandson James for the first time. As I cuddled him I felt so very privileged and I realised this was such a precious moment. The rush of love I experienced was one that only a grandmother can experience.

Now three years later, still words cannot express the most special emotion I feel for my grandson.

---o-O-o---

Katherine Owen

Poet, writer, member of Swindon's Bluegate Poets group.

Journeying

The spiritual journey is so rich with so many new beginnings. One of these for me was the moment when I moved forward in understanding that I was not waiting for God to help me. Instead, God was waiting for my invitation to be and act in my life. We can think that we have to change before we are worthy of God and it just isn't true. We need to invite God into whatever is happening in our life right now. We need to open our minds to give Him/Her/It access to help us.

I was severely disabled for many years with ME/CFS. Though I wouldn't wish it on anyone, it led me to put my roots down into awareness of God, Light, Energy, Presence, the Divine – the names don't matter, they really don't matter. The experience of Love and Guidance is now a part of every day of my life, and for this I am profoundly grateful.

I Am Only Waiting

You are waiting for the perfect time,
the perfect space within which to
welcome me;

Waiting for the right teacher to
give you
the right words,
the right rituals;

Waiting until you are alone or
until you are with others;

Waiting…
to be good enough,
to be ready,
to feel the way
you should feel;

Waiting until you can give me
the respect I deserve.

Do not treat me with such reverence.
Do you not know that I am in
everything –
the sacred and the profane,
the worthy and the unworthy?

Do you not know that
I am already in
you?

The time is right when
you say it is.
The time is right
now.

Do you not understand:
I am only awaiting
your invitation?

Linzey Bell

34, married mother of two, hard worker, determined to love life!

New Paths

I really am not sure how I begin to explain to you why I decided to change the path I was on and why I decided to take a Spiritual approach on my life. But I will try, and hopefully you may take something away from reading this that might inspire your life in someway.

I am thirty four, married to the man I fell in love with at fifteen, and although he annoys me sometimes, he is still the love of my life. We have two children, my son who is thirteen and my daughter who is eight. They fight like cat and dog but love each other anyway. Pretty normal for most siblings I suppose. My marriage hasn't been without its problems. Some much worse than others but we scrambled our way through every one, somehow. Probably partly to do with my stubborn streak and the fact that I hate being defeated.

I was brought up well and was taught many old-fashioned values; one being that once you are married you don't just give up on it because things get slightly too tough. You get married, you have children, you have responsibilities. You keep your family safe and secure and you commit to that wholeheartedly.

13

But I'm no saint. I've had low points in my life. I've derailed, made mistakes, lost my path. I began to question what I was becoming. I was so busy wallowing in my own self-pity. I had forgotten what was important. I had forgotten how to be my real happy, laid back, life loving me. When I looked in the mirror I didn't like what I could see. Who was I? So I decided to change my path. 'If you don't like something Linzey, change it', I told myself. I was the only who could. As individuals we hold the key to change the direction our lives might take. Life is all about choices.

I started to go to Spiritual Church. It was something I had always been curious about. I needed some form of answer. I wasn't even sure if I would get any answers but I needed something – and I found it. It enlightened me. It made me realise we are all looking for answers, reassurance. No matter what walk of life you come from, we all need guidance.

My Spiritual path gave me the reassurance I needed. It made me feel positive. I realised that as a family we have hardly any money, but what we have we work hard for. We are healthy and we love each other. The Spiritual path I took changed my whole outlook on life. I'm proud that I had the strength to alter the direction I was going in. I decided that I would do things that would continue to make me happy. I managed to get in touch with my childhood friend who I grew up with from a very early age till I was nineteen. We had lost contact for thirteen years but now I speak to her frequently and get together often. I'm overjoyed. She is important to me. I discovered her life had also hit a low point. She also took the spiritual route.

I now have so many positives in my life I no longer have time to dwell on the negatives – you reap what you sow – and all that. Life owes us nothing. The world owes us nothing. It is what you make it. Don't complain. Change it. I'm not sure if what I told you makes sense to anyone apart from me, but just remember you have a choice. You have a choice on whether you make things better, to make life positive.

Catherine Elliott

Born Rochdale, Lancashire, now living in Leamington Spa Warwickshire. Happily married with two boys in their late twenties. One living in Manchester, the other in Hong Kong

A Different Kind of Nurturing

Fear holds so many people back from doing what they really would like to do, and it seems to be one of those things that many women put on the back burner, as so many other things, which they may consider to be more important, are happening in their lives.

When I retired early, thanks to a very understanding husband, after a very exciting teaching career I fancied a complete change. Peace instead of hectic activity, calmness instead of stress, quietness instead of the noise of young children, and time to think and reflect. Time to simply be me, to work outside, close to nature. The only sound to accompany my hard work was birdsong, and occasionally when I fancied it, Radio Four.

It was indeed a new beginning.

I made fliers which I posted through doors (especially those who had gardens that I could see needed a little T.L.C.) and in the meantime a close friend asked if I would redesign her garden. This kept me busy initially, and whilst I was weeding her front garden, a lady passed by and asked if I gardened for a living. When I told her I did, she asked me to call in at her address, and having done just that a week later I had client number two! It is surprising how many people are on the look out for help, and need a trustworthy person that they feel safe to employ. She was an elderly lady, so being a woman, perhaps I fitted the bill of not being a threat.

A few weeks later and I had a telephone call from a family who had read my flier, and were looking for help in the garden. This was the start up of client number three. I had decided that although I was fairly fit, that working two hours each morning was sufficient, and this still left me time to go to yoga classes, have a swim, and enjoy my retirement. Friday was strictly out of bounds for any work, as it was my day shared with friends.

I hadn't had horticultural training, but I had had a long interest in gardening, and had taken on an allotment when my two sons started school, so I was used to digging and hard work. I read a great deal about the subject, looked in gardening magazines, tried out many plants in my own garden, and experimented with which shapes, colours and textures that blend well together. I learnt day by day over many years, and although I have had shrubs grow too large, most of my planting has survived, and indeed thrived. The very few losses over the past twelve years happened this winter when extreme cold, and long spells of snow did cause me to loose two Ceanothus. Talking of new beginnings however, the Ceanothus has fought back, and after a severe pruning, (my not wanting to give up on any plant until it was certain that it really was dead!) I found two teeny weenie little green sprouting buds on the lower branches... so perhaps all is not lost.

Certain things have not changed in my outlook to gardening. I'm not a lover of lawns, although I mow two every week. They give my client and friend a lot of pleasure, and it is their garden, so my personal taste has to take a back seat. I hate rows, and uniformity. I love drifts, woodland glades and bulbs, so my gardens from February to May are heaven.

Planting is for now, but it is also for the future, and although my husband and two sons, whilst being supportive, cannot really share my delight in nurture, growth and flowering... it isn't perhaps a million miles away from what I was trained to do all those years ago. It was a new beginning, but now that I've written this down maybe it is simply the class that changed!

Just living my life

JUST LIVING MY LIFE

Angela Kennedy

Born in London to Irish parents. Retired teacher.
Happily married for forty years and mother of three children.
Lived in Highworth for thirty-five years.

Flexible Living

Each day I get up about 7.30am and after breakfast catch up on the national and local news. After this we (my husband and I) walk up to Highworth for a paper and visit a few shops. I usually meet quite a few people for a chat and then progress to the local library. Here things are looked up on the internet, magazines read and I check out the new books. Home then for a coffee and a read of the paper. General household jobs and telephone calls are usually done at this time. The afternoons are varied and may involve going to visit a new place; visiting my elderly friend in a nursing home; catching up with a neighbour or some gardening when the weather permits.

I love the flexibility of my life and the fact that each day can be so different. Sometimes I'll meet up with ex-teaching colleagues and friends for a chat. At other times I go to London, tend my parents' grave and then visit my sister to spend time with her. Now and again we go to the south coast to stay with our son – this is great as he lives on the sea-front. We also look forward to visiting our daughters, sons-in-law and grandchildren and having them stay here as well. My hobbies are reading and knitting and I love browsing around antique and collectable shops. I very much appreciate my fitness and mobility and that nothings restricts what I may want to do. I like to think I am keeping myself fit and eating healthily in readiness for the 'golden years'

So I feel very happy with how I am living my life. I hope I look out for, and am there for, those who may need help. Having spent twelve years travelling to London to care for my parents in conjunction with my sister, I now really appreciate holidays away, days out and unexpected treats. We don't travel abroad because there are so many places we want to visit in the U.K. and Ireland and sometimes, there are not enough hours in the day. Sometimes I panic about not being able to read all the books on my list.

Now to the most important part of all – I had wonderful parents and a very happy childhood. I have a lovely family now and my day is always complete when it includes prayer and communication with God. Taking part in the Mass each Sunday is very important to me and I believe it has been pivotal in my personal development.

Retirement has been really good so far. I think people my age were born at just the right time because:

· we can chose to take the bus or drive;
· we can buy a ready meal or produce a home cooked one;
· we can send an e-mail or write a letter to friends;
· we can enjoy a lovely hotel break or a self-catering holiday;
· we can go to the cinema or watch a DVD at home;

never has there been so much choice!

I hope this gives you some insight into my life at present – I have so much to be grateful for.

Mary Crichton

61 years, divorced, lived in Highworth about fifteen years.

Chopsticks and Other Things!

Kneeling in the undergrowth of my small garden, I'm doing battle with a sort of dead nettle with yellow flowers; I'll call it the 'thingy' plant! (I'm sure I knew the name once upon a time but it escapes me now – senior moment?) I'm musing that now just retired, I should have time to tame this beast. Yet I mustn't complain; 'thingy' plant covers a multitude of sins and it grows where nothing else will. The trouble is 'thingy' plant never wants to be contained and sends out tendrils at remarkable speed invading the rest of the garden. But let me tell you the real point of this rambling: not three feet from me landed a lovely red-breasted robin intent on exploring the ground laid bare and it didn't even budge when I threw him a juicy caterpillar – how magical was that! I may have reached that 'Third Age' (ghastly term) but I still have a childlike thrill when seeing wildlife at such close quarters!

The other side of the garden, the ex is preparing to drill a three inch long hole in my neighbour's wall. I really should have asked the neighbour first but it seemed more urgent to use the ex's skills whilst he's visiting. I really do need to get the bracket fixed to the wall from which to hang four rather heavy terracotta pots that my medical student daughter gave me. She will expect to see them hanging on her next flying visit. She announced said flying visit earlier in the day, an opportune visit to see both parents at one go so to speak. Mind you, I understand given the breath-taking speed of her course, that putting up a bracket for terracotta pots is a minor operation. Just the other day, she announced she's practising suturing a pig's trotter. The next day, I get a text telling me she's been sewing up a patient! I suppose this is everyday learning for her but it leaves me flabbergasted. Like "tying knots with chopsticks" she tells me and "it's so cool!"

This brings me to a book I've just finished about girls growing up in rural China – not so cool! Girls there are referred to as chopsticks; useful but dispensable. Boys on the other hand are said to be like beams holding up a house; strong and indispensable. A family without sons is considered so unlucky that some mothers have committed suicide because they have not produced sons! It reminds me there are still many parts of the world where women's emancipation has a long way to go. Thank heavens my daughter hasn't had such difficulties.

Returning to the 'thingy' plant and musing on the chopstick girls, I feel very fortunate not to have been contained either and I have had choices and opportunities that women a generation ago never had and many in rural China still lack. I have travelled widely, obtained a degree, enjoyed a career and have three lovely children. The Pill, kitchen appliances and our society have freed women like me and I feel very blessed. And I am not finished yet. I am now able to live independently (and I do appreciate the ex's visits and am glad we still get on so well). There are so many things I'd like to do and more importantly, now retired, I can spend more time with my friends and family – including the ex! – I only hope they won't mind!

Pat Elkington

Married, mother and grandmother; needlewoman of many years, bridge player, interested in Fine Arts, live in Highworth, Wiltshire.

Sewing Times

It's finished! It's finished! It's finally finished! I have put positively the last stitch into my part of a project I have been working on for two years!

It all started two years ago – well, no, a lot longer than that, really. Let's go back to when our daughter got married – empty nest – so I decided to sign up for a GCSE embroidery course, only by the time it got under way it had metamorphosed into a City and Guilds course. So after five years, I had scraped a pass and mastered all the embroidery techniques known to womankind. Obviously!

A few months later we moved to Wiltshire, and it was not long before I was roped in to take part in a project to create a festival set for the beautiful, historic church at Fairford.

My first taste of real ecclesiastical embroidery. Heart-stopping as we used the best quality gold threads on unbelievably expensive fabric. I only did a part of the work, so feel I can admit that the overall result was spectacular.

The years rolled by until two years ago, when two members of our small embroidery group wished to replace a Lent/Advent set for their church. A set comprises an Altar frontal, orphreys, superfrontal, lectern and pulpit falls, burse and veil, so we decided to make it a group project.

It was immense fun comparing and compiling designs, putting them before the Vicar and PCC, then choosing fabrics (purple) and threads and working out quantities. Then the hard work began. I became responsible for the frontal. Painstaking work on a big frame takes care and attention, and very good light. By the time I had finished it, although I had been a motive force in the planning I threw my hat in the air, declared to anybody who would listen that I would never, ever, undertake such a large piece of work again, and gave my big frame to the charity shop. However, I did relent far enough to undertake the veil – a very small part indeed of the whole set, but now that is completed as well, and I can relax!

Next week I take it to the lady who is doing the making up for us, and the Dedication will be early next month. My life opens up before me again – I do not have to feel guilty if I just sit in the garden or in front of the TV. I might even make a couple of things for my dolls house! Or really annoy my husband by embarking on another cushion – his pet hate!

But wait, he has a hopeful expression in his eyes – he thinks I now have time to mend a couple of trouser pockets! Well, they do say the devil makes work for idle hands.

Julia Falaki

Lived in Swindon for 19 years. Married with three children. Have worked for the private, public and voluntary sectors. For many years have been committed to supporting the local community – currently an LEA primary school governor, chair of the Swindon Businesswomen's Breakfast Club. Self-employed, offering project management in the adult learning sector.

Juggling

Three children, ranging in age from twelve to nineteen, dictate much of what my day consists of, as all those with children will recognise. Now that my youngest catches the bus to school (just opposite where we live), and I try to instil a sense of independence in all of them, she has to get herself up, get ready and leave the house in time to catch the bus. This means, that unless I have an early meeting, I am not tied to my alarm clock. Getting up for me is a huge feat of self-discipline. I am not an early morning person, love the comfort of my bed, and my husband knows not to have any in-depth conversation with me before I have been up and running for at least two hours.

Where possible, I book meetings for 10am, giving me some incentive to haul myself up and get going. However, one of my contracts does mean I have to get up and out of the house by 8.30am, otherwise I will never find a parking space.

Ever since my son was born, over 19 years ago, I made the decision that I didn't want to work full-time ever again. So far this has worked, even though I am now self-employed. At one stage I took on too much work, and after much stress and working into the evenings, I decided again that enough was enough and that I would say "no" to extra work.

I work very flexibly. When I took on my current contracts I explained that I wanted flexible hours of working and in return, I will be available by 'phone or email most of the time. I count how many hours I work each week and it is swings and roundabouts. Some weeks I work more than the contracted hours, and others are less.

When the children were younger I had very naively thought that as they got older, they would need me less. How wrong could I be? With one at university and two still at school, extra-curricular activities during both day and evening, plus work, mean that some days I am a yoyo in and out of the house.

I had also naively told the children that they could each have two extra-curricular activities per week only. This works well, if the activities are one hour hobbies per week, but not when they take over your life because they are elite at sports or music. And suddenly those weekends you kept free are full of competitions, lessons because you can't fit them in the rest of the week, festivals and rehearsals.

Oh, and I forgot, I am also a school governor, chair of a local businesswomen's networking club, and have applied to be a volunteer at the Olympics.

So for me, no two days are alike, nor the weekends. I sometimes wonder what life would be like if my children didn't do any extra-curricular activities, like several of my friends' children, and if I worked set hours per week, or dare I say it, worked full-time. Although I am in my middle-age, I cannot see myself not working and not running around. So once the children have all 'grown up' and left home to lead their own lives, I would love to do more voluntary work and go out more with my husband, otherwise my bed will become my best friend.

Malathy Sitaram

A voracious reader with a passionate interest in politics and current affairs. The passion extends to ideas, food and cookery. My idea of a perfect evening is good food in the company of good talkers with plenty of argument and humour.

The Indian Shop

The highlight of my week is my visit to the Indian shop on Wednesday mornings. We call it the Indian shop although it and several others on the street are run by persons of Pakistani or Bangladeshi origin. It is Indian as far as we are concerned because it sells Indian vegetables and seasonal fruit, Indian spices and an array of different lentils. In short, everything needed for an Indian meal.

Shopping there is a highlight because I love being in the midst of fellow Indians, some of whom I may know and above all I get a chance to speak Hindi, the national language of India but superseded by English for me as I attended Anglo-Indian schools. I hardly ever spoke Hindi in India. It took third place in school, after English and the second language, French. Indians normally speak more than one language of which there are eighteen in India and hundreds of dialects.

Ah, the joy of speaking Hindi to the man at the till. Joy because I did not know that I could speak it. The brain whose mysteries have not been fully fathomed has secreted in some part of it, a memory of the language which I hardly ever used in India, as all my friends spoke English. How do I know these words I ask myself? What neural pathway facilitates this strange fluency? And why do I feel so happy using it, when I had felt so superior speaking only English in India being, as I am, a casualty of colonialism? Some of the few Indian friends I have here are Hindi speakers. With them I dry up and cannot speak fluently. In the shop, most people do not know who I am and perhaps this is what spurs me on.

The most common language heard in the shop is Gujerati, reflecting the huge influx of Gujeratis from Africa in the 1970s. There are also Punjabi speakers, plenty of newly arrived Goans speaking Konkani and some people from South India with its variety of languages, one of which is supposed to be my mother tongue! Bengalis too. For the half hour that I spend in the shop I feel quite serendipitous, transported as I am to a miniature India with all the noise and linguistic babble. I don't think that in India I would feel similarly exhilarated because I am not in the minority there. There's a thought.

23

Fresh produce arrives on Wednesday morning. A man goes at dawn to a huge market in Southall, not far from Heathrow, fills up his van, drives back and lays out the boxes of fresh veg and fruit in a line on the shop floor by 9a.m. These shops are usually very small, lined with shelves that are packed with tins and packets and jars. An aroma of dry spices hangs over the shop. The freezers are packed with tropical fish without which Bangladeshis cannot live and nowadays we get excellent frozen parathas and chappatis and samosas all made in the UK. In a back room, a butcher sells meat and chicken but not pork.

I aim to get there by 9.15 and fill my basket with fresh green coriander, spinach, green chillies, limes, and vegetables that you would not recognize. We are in the main vegetarian and so I am delighted that Indian veggies are available. From April to July, the shop is crowded because it is the mango season; there is almost a scrimmage to get at the nectar bearing boxes Crates of Alphonso mangoes from India and other equally delicious varieties from Pakistan, such as Kesar, fill the shop with their heavenly aroma that titillates the senses with its promise of imminent luscious delight. Most of us will indulge in an orgy of eating mangoes for at least two months. Every morning at breakfast, I eat one large, luscious, golden orange fruit right through May, June and July and feel the better for it. It is packed with vitamins. Over indulgence though can lead to the inevitable result. In India, my mother would say that too many mangoes would overheat the body and cause boils.

The owner of the shop is a Muslim but several of the religious festivals of India are celebrated here with special sweetmeats brought from London to celebrate Diwali, Eid and Christmas. Generally the shoppers look cheerful and are not in a hurry as I usually am. I fit in this half hour early in the day, pleased that I have obtained the vegetables my mother prepared so well long, long ago and which will see us through for another week.

Nicola Hudson

55. Bird Rescuer. Lives in Somerset.

'Alonso Cheep'

One May day my son came cycling furiously up the drive and ran in doors calling "Mum, Mum". In his hand he held a small fluffy bundle. The fluffy bundle was brown and speckled with beady eyes. He said he had found it in the road 1.5 miles away and it couldn't fly. I told him he should have left it where it was because the parent bird would look after it – this was before I inspected it. I found it had a large hole in its back and was bleeding. I did the usual thing – found a suitable box to calm it down and see if it survived the night. I really didn't hold out much hope – the hole in its back was large and it had totally lost the use of the leg on the same side.

Next morning, I went, in trepidation, to see if it was still alive. It was so, I gave it fresh water and started trying to teach it to eat 'blobs'. Blobs are a dried puppy food which is suitable to feed meat eating birds – it has all the right goodness and I have found them perfect in the past for rearing these types of birds. I started to push small bits of blobs down the throat of this tiny bundle. The first day is always difficult but after that they usually take to the new diet well. This little bird could only stand on one leg and the other appeared to dangle and go in all directions – it also became hot and swollen over the coming days. After a lot of care and taking the bird to work with me in order to feed it as often as its parent would, I began to believe it may survive. Two weeks pass and I was soaking its bad leg in salty water twice a day, its appetite grew and soon it learnt to pick up the food itself. The leg grew stronger – it didn't go off in all directions. Sadly the little toes on that foot dropped off and he was left with stumps but eventually he could bear weight and hold on to my finger with his foot. I then named him as Alonso Cheep.

Alonso Cheep was free in the kitchen and when dusk began to fall he would fly up onto the rechargeable torch and roost. I could then pick him down and put him in a cage for the night in order that my cat could sleep in her normal bed in the kitchen!

We taught Alonso to fly to us in order to be fed and when he could do that we decided the time had come to let him outside – none of us agree with bird or animals being caged. We took him into the garden and let him scratch about in the flower bed for food. He flew into the lower branches of the tree and then came back to us for more food. At night he came indoors again to go to bed. After about a week we let him stay out in the garden for good. The first night a tremendous storm blew up – thunder, lightening, torrential rain and strong winds. The next morning there was no sign of Alonso. It was heartbreaking. Everyday I got up and went out to call him but he never came back.

It had upset me so much that one night I had a dream about him. I woke in the morning and told my husband of this vivid dream where I had seen Alonso sitting in the drive and I jumped out of bed to look out of the window – the dream was so real. This was two weeks after the storm and there in the middle of the drive was a blackbird. I ran down the stairs and out of the front door calling him but not really expecting it to be Alonso. The bird never flew away and let me go right up to him and pick him up. He came indoors and ate a hearty breakfast. In those two weeks he had grown up and proved he was quite capable of looking after himself. He then lived in the garden all winter – singing outside the back door. My cat never attempted to catch him. The following spring he found a mate and brought her into the garden – they made a nest and had four chicks which they taught to eat blobs thrown out by the 'people in the house'. They had a second clutch of chicks in a second nest built in the pyracantha hedge. Again their offspring ate blobs.

Alonso went off during that winter but returned again the following spring – singing outside the back door and allowing me to touch him. He was a little less bright and cheerful. Then I never saw him again. On reading up about blackbirds I found that their normal age is two years.

I feel privileged to have been able to give that wonderful bird a life which he would otherwise not have had and for him to have had that life as a free bird. I will never forget him.

Liz Gibney

52, from Swindon. Have lived in Swindon for about 25 years – I came here when I married but spent about four years away.

The Empty Nest

Today, I awoke again to an empty house. I crawled out of bed, made some tea, crawled back into bed and settled for a short read. It is before 7am. In the next hour I will have breakfast, get washed and dressed, do a few odd jobs and leave for work. Not so long ago, I would have leaped out of bed just before 8am, rushed around getting three children ready for school – tying laces, brushing hair, finding books, making breakfasts and finally seen them safely out of the door, all in approximately one hour! But now, it is just me – unless my husband is home from work and then he languishes in bed, usually until I leave the house.

I work in a secondary school as a Teaching Assistant, which means that I work with children who are 11–16 years old and have special needs: often dyslexia or nowadays, more frequently, with children who have ASD (Autistic Spectrum Disorder). These children are in 'normal' classes and learn alongside other children their age. I mostly work in English classes, which I really enjoy as I like books and like to learn things that I did not come across in my liberal 1960's and 70's education! The pace is frenetic; everything about education today seems to go at top speed. The school is awash with technology; everything seems to be all-singing, all-dancing. But my favourite lessons are when we read a novel. Who can not enjoy being drawn into a good story?

I am regularly amazed by the children I work with. Amazed by their knowledge (or lack of it), amazed by their observations ("why do you always push the wrong door, Miss?"), surprised by their experiences and again, surprised by how some lead such narrow lives. I enjoy watching them grow up ("I'm going to start to work this year, Miss") and I enjoy being asked if I'm their friend and sharing their stories. Don't get me wrong, it is not all sunshine. There are times when my patience is stretched and I am disappointed and exhausted by pupils. But most of all, I love it when you can make something clear, when you can explain something that has been a problem and the 'penny eventually drops'.

The school day ends and I'm dying for a cup of tea. The 'empty nest' isn't so daunting and it appears to be rapidly filling up. I have chosen to work an extra day. I seem to get home later than ever... I don't have to come back on time anymore. The house stays clean, I choose the TV station, the radio is permanently tuned to Radio 4 and not to a station blaring banal trivialities, I eat when I want and what I want, I gossip on the phone and have taken back ownership of my life. I go to the gym, I am an active member of my church and enjoy walking. I am also learning to cook less. I know that this may not last: there are aging parents and broody daughters, not to mention those unforeseen circumstances that sneak up on us at times. But at the moment, this interlude in my life is just fine.

Kathleen Bentley

73, mother, grandmother and great-grandmother.

TLC

Last night I had a night carer which happens three times a week. For once I was still asleep at 7.30 when two lovely cheerful morning carers arrived to get up my husband Ron who has Parkinsons and Dementia. At Christmas when my visiting son-in-law was awoken at their arrival, he sat up grumpily in bed and said, "Well I've never met them, but they must be called Bright and Cheerful!"

The carers showered and dressed Ron and brought him through for breakfast.

I recently had my bathroom changed to a wet room with a lovely power shower which is so much easier for us both. It has been a good morning. Ron even got up unaided from his reclining chair and walked to the kitchen. He usually needs help for everything so this was so encouraging.

All over the house we have alarms for fire, food, gas, falls and 'out of bed for 15 minutes' pressure mats. The marvellously helpful rep from 'Careline' who came this lunchtime even offered something to be worn called 'tilt and fall' for both of us, as I've had more falls than Ron lately. Fortunately yesterday I did not break either teeth, glasses or nose, just my pride. Several bits ache and are not working as normal today.

My youngest daughter is over from Ireland for a week's visit. It is amazing how much difference an extra pair of hands makes. She supervised her dad's dinner today as, although he was able to feed himself, it's a messy process. She also helped him to the toilet and made drinks.

I'm thankful that so far today nothing has broken down or other disaster discovered. We had so many things go wrong from minor breakages and breakdowns to the total collapse of the drains. I mistakenly said at the ladies prayer meeting "I've had so many men just lately!" I was laughingly asked if I would please rephrase that!

This is such a contrast from the days when my husband was strong and able to tackle, make or mend most things, not only for us but for all the neighbours and friends.

I am really grateful for all the support we have from all the services; medical, social, support workers etc. The girls the social services send in to help obviously care about Ron and myself and their job.

My other two daughters live nearby and are a wonderful support in spite of having families and busy jobs. Friends are a support and encouragement. If any of you read this, then thank you with all my heart for keeping me going. One granddaughter regularly pops in after college with a bag of chips to share with granddad and I love to see my other seven grandchildren and three great-grandchildren when they visit.

The day finished very peacefully and I went to bed as soon as Ron was tucked up.

Life is very different now and sometimes is quite a challenge. We are Christians and I am so thankful that I have a hope to cling onto when the going is rough.

Dr. Linda Wilson

56. Senior Lecturer in Theology by Distance Learning, University of Gloucestershire. Originally from Stockport but last forty years in Bristol. Married.

A Typical Day

It is a sunny morning in March, and I am looking out of my window at the gardens and houses behind, and at one of my cats picking her way carefully along the fence before leaping down into a neighbour's garden. I am at my computer, following the usual morning routine: checking emails, making a few quick comments on Facebook, then taking a few minutes to reflect and pray, before dealing with work. My work is a mixture: teaching church history by distance learning, tutoring students on an MA in church leadership, planning a meeting for our home-based church, doing my own research and writing.

Sometimes there are essays to mark, or online seminars to engage with; sometimes there are students or friends to email or phone, but this day I am planning out some research into the lives of women in the early nineteenth and twentieth centuries in Bristol. Spider diagrams and lists, a rough timetable (which of course I won't keep to), books to read. The actual research I love: sitting in the record office, with the book, on its special pillow, opening it with anticipation. Will it be just tedious or worse, illegible accounts of endless meetings, or will there be little gems, indications of character, glimpses of what was important to these women, what their lives were really like? In the middle of the minutes of temperance meetings in East Bristol, a few weeks ago, I suddenly discovered a petition to the local MP in support of women's suffrage. Planning, I hope for more such moments.

In the middle of this it is time for coffee: my husband and I, both working from home in our respective studies, randomly take it in turns to bring each other sustaining drink and nibbles. Today I am meeting a friend for lunch. I walk along the river in the centre of Bristol, talking to the swans. Over a tasty bowl of mushroom soup we catch up, compare notes, enjoy each other's company. I reach home again, planning a return to the computer, but my daughter phones: the grandchildren want to see me, can they pop over? So they come, drinks are made, paper and coloured pencils come out for my granddaughter, cars for my little grandson. Later, I am babysitting for them. I take a pile of books, both work and leisure, and also ponder the difficult question of next week, how many eggs will be needed for the pancake party we are planning next week for friends and neighbours? I try and work it out, I go up and downstairs to my granddaughter several times, then retreat into a sci-fi novel. Home at the end of all that, my husband and I end the day by chatting a bit, then burying ourselves in our respective books, easy in each others' company after over 35 years.

This is a typical day: a mixture of work, friendship, family. They leak into each other, and I enjoy that. Of course there are heartaches, concerns about people and about church, things that could be different… but I am at peace. It was a good day.

Tessa Disney

23. Shrivenham born and bred.

This is My Life

I wake up. And I go to sleep. This is my life.

It's full, that's true and indisputable, with great family who are always there, never judging nor deceitful, just full of love. With amazing friends who have lasted through the years, endless cups of tea and shoulders galore.

A home. My home. Though there have been many other places I have laid my hat in my relatively short life, there really is no place…

I am not sick, unloved, homeless or poor, or indeed any of the other million things that we attribute to unhappiness.

So, therefore I'm happy. Right?

A day. This day. Yesterday, tomorrow – all quite indistinguishable at present.

I read a lot. Finding solace in that centuries old art of escapism. More content to be lost in a world someone else has created than my own, seriously lacking world I seem to have no control over.

I know, we all know, exactly what's going to happen in each and every one of these books I read. There are always tricks, trials and tribulations along the way but ultimately I read them for what I know will happen in the end. Always. Eventually.

And this is my life. A day, weeks, months and years have gone by already. A different city, different job, new chapter – same story.

I live, and I wait. Searching for my happily ever after.

The End.

Teresa Clare Nestor

Born and live in Swindon Town. Single.

Tuesdays

My Tuesdays only start when my alarm clock has sounded its screeching tones AND has been snoozed for about the third time – I'm not happy about leaving my nice, warm bed, and always get dressed in a zombie like fashion.

The next most important thing after that is the radio – I always put that on in the mornings, even if I'm running late (which is not unheard of!). Even if it's not something I would normally choose to listen to, I have to hear music in the background; I've always loved a variety of music.

I'm currently unemployed and looking for a job and one of the ways I do this is by using the internet at the Swindon Central Library. I know at the moment the employment situation isn't good for anyone, but a job isn't just going to plonk itself in my lap is it? Besides, it gets me out of the house and into sort of a routine – anyway: you never know who you might meet there! As the days are getting a bit better weather-wise now, I usually have a cup of tea out in their courtyard too. But only if it's nice – I like heat! I've got bad circulation due to my disability, so I blame it on that!

From there I go into the town. I'm in a wheelchair and I always want to laugh when I roll down the slope outside the library – because my wheels make such a rattle on the uneven concrete it makes people turn their heads, and then they suddenly get a look of horror on their faces when they see me hurtling towards them! I haven't hit anyone yet though – I think I know what I'm doing. (But I'm touching wood as I type this… you know, just in case!)

Small children are funny when they see me. I don't think it's that often they see someone sitting in something with huge wheels – but that isn't actually a car! Although I have to say, it can sometimes be quite hazardous: I can immediately think of at least three occasions where a small boy or girl has stared so intensely that they have ended up crashing into a bollard or a display stand because they were walking and gawping at the same time! I don't laugh out loud when they do this – well, at least I haven't yet! But I do think it's quite sweet really. It's not always so funny when they're with their parents because the parents get embarrassed and tell them not to look – but it doesn't bother me. Now and then some kids will just come right out with it and ask why I'm not walking like them – I'd much rather that then parents or the adult that they're with making them feel like it's a bad thing to stare and wonder about it. I just tell them my legs aren't as strong as theirs.

Anyway, when I come out of the library I usually have some lunch before going back home – but not before I've brought some milk for tea – I have to make sure I've got that because I do drink a lot of it!

Then next in the day is the laundry. I do try to get excited about laundry and housework – trying to pretend that I'm getting a workout or something – but the enthusiasm is very short lived I can tell you! My get out clause with that job is my neighbour, if I see her then that can sometimes be the afternoon gone! Actually if I thought about it, I couldn't tell you what takes so long to talk about but obviously we always manage to find something! But she is really nice so it's good to find out what she's up to.

I'm a really big fan of the Vampire Diaries. I tell you this because on a Tuesday night I don't let anything get in the way of watching that programme. I love it, and I make sure EVERYTHING is done before I settle down to watch it.

Frances 'Fran' Bevan

57. Londoner but have now lived in Swindon for last 23 years.. Married with children. Historical journalist for local paper amongst other things.

Day 210 of my 'Gap Year'

There was no such thing as a gap year in my youth – that fun filled twelve month period of freedom most students take between sitting A level examinations and beginning university. But then university wasn't for the likes of me.

My parents allowed me to remain at school for an extra year to sit CSE exams, the forerunner of the GCSE. Introduced by a Labour government in 1965, the Certificate of Secondary Education provided Secondary School leavers with a qualification. Although inferior to the GCE 'O' level, it was better than nothing.

I started work shortly before my 16th birthday in August 1969. Both my parents had entered the workforce at fourteen so I could consider myself lucky, they told me.

I wanted to be a writer but mum settled for letting me start work as an office junior on the local weekly newspaper, the Haverhill Echo, her one concession to my aspirations. She wanted me to get a job in a bank.

Two marriages, three children, approximately ten jobs and forty one years later, I have decided to take a gap year. To do what, exactly? Write.

With three weekly articles on local and family history for the Swindon Advertiser, I am also working on an account of the life and times of a Swindon born Suffragette. Edith New famously broke windows at 10 Downing Street during the increasingly militant suffrage campaign in the early part of the 20th century, but is largely unknown in the town of her birth.

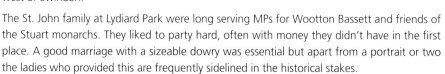

Another of my projects is a series of short biographies on the Ladies of Lydiard, the consorts of those important 18th century gentlemen who owned the North Wiltshire property at Lydiard Tregoze, west of Swindon.

The St. John family at Lydiard Park were long serving MPs for Wootton Bassett and friends of the Stuart monarchs. They liked to party hard, often with money they didn't have in the first place. A good marriage with a sizeable dowry was essential but apart from a portrait or two the ladies who provided this are frequently sidelined in the historical stakes.

So how did I spend day 210 of my gap year. By eight o'clock I was at my computer, answering emails and working on some online research.

By midday I was in the Central Library Swindon for the launch of the 18th Swindon Festival of Literature, merely as a spectator, but who knows – one day!

Then armed with a sandwich and a bottle of water I headed for Radnor Street Cemetery. I spent the afternoon in glorious sunshine photographing some of the magnificent Victorian monuments for inclusion in a promotional pamphlet.

Closed to new burials in the 1970s the cemetery has suffered from neglect and vandalism in recent years and is badly in need of recognition. As a member of the Friends of Radnor Street Cemetery we are set to change all that with guided walks of the historically important cemetery and exhibitions in the chapel.

Back home to upload the photographs on to my computer and more research.

Like those students enjoying their freedom, life may get more serious come September. But for now, bring on day 211 of my gap year!

Evelyn Heasman

*Live in Stanton Fitzwarren with three of my five children.
I have a degree in Environmental Management and a passion for
African Drumming. I am not very good at frills and detail –
fact, logic and common sense, tempered heavily by an inability to detect
when someone lies, or to understand most jokes.*

No Lists!

This morning I am trying to break the habit of a decades – lists – writing lists – of work to be done, jobs to be started, projects to be completed, which seeds to sow, vegetables to tend, meals to cook, ingredients to purchase, bills to pay, places to visit, relatives to telephone!

The house needs cleaning, the tyres of the van need replacing and I need to make a dental appointment. There are e.mails to check and reply to, linen to iron, floors to mop, and wood to chop for the fire.

Fortunately I do not spend time watching television. I haven't joined the cults of consumerism and celebrity worship and have little interest in technology. So call ME old fashioned!! Neither do I bother much with painting my nails or straightening my hair, going to the health spa or beauty salon There just isn't time – my lists are long… I grow my own organic vegetables and really enjoy reading about conspiracy theories. I believe them all!

So, just for today – I am going to ignore my lists – I will live the day and write about it as it unfolds.

7am   My eldest daughter brings me a lovely cup of coffee and a couple of digestives and tries not to trip on the boxes of books and thirty plus African drums that are squeezed into the room.

7.10am I start a quick tidy around the house – open all the windows and doors – say "hello" to the cats.

8am   I am busy, with the help of my sixteen year old, wrapping parcels to send to Australia – vintage salt and pepper shakers to a collector of Sadler ware.

9am   Now at the post office, weighing parcels and calculating costs, then a quick visit next door to the chemist for some hair dye. I can't decide on the colour and leave empty handed.

10am   Returned home to do some laundry and bake some bread – finish off writing letters to my family in Ireland and Cornwall and pop them in the post box at the end of my garden.

11am   Pick some peas and lettuce from the vegetable garden for lunch. I will cook some rice and add onion, peas, spices and nuts.

12 noon   The post has arrived – another bill for gas and electric – so expensive.

This afternoon I have repaired and sewn up some tears in three pairs of trousers and groomed the cats to prevent fleas taking hold.

A quick visit to the library for a book on antiques. Home, kettle on and read a few chapters, then into the garden to pick some cabbage and kale to go with the purple potatoes I grew this year. I will pop to my neighbour later and swap my potatoes for some jam.

Well, I haven't made any lists today, the sun has just about set and the dinner is still cooking. Hopefully I still have time to clear out the store cupboard ready for the pots of jam and chutney to be made later in the year.

I often hear myself saying "there's not enough time in the day" and I look back to when I had five young children to care for – the days seemed long – I did less housework – I had time for myself – to read… to listen to plays on the radio..

Maybe tomorrow!

Hilda Sheehan

(sometimes Mabel Watson)

Writer, literature development worker and editor of 'Domestic Cherry' magazine.

Will I Drown in My Own...?

Will I drown in my own washing basket before my first book, if I am so lucky, floats up to the great heights of a shelf in Waterstones wearing a life jacket?

Currently I am a full time stay at home mum with five young people to care for including three year old twins. Looking around me this morning I see a pile of last night's and this morning's washing up, a mountain of washing (excuse the cliché there *are* no other words!), two undressed toddlers (it's nearly ten o'clock but they are smiling and playing) some spilt Cheerios, a mucky floor, some walls that should have been decorated, carpets that should be hoovered and I could go on. The trouble is on top of all of this I am a full time writer and developer of all things poetry in Swindon and further afield. I manage this without even an hour's child care or family support. I think this is very common with today's women; we can do so much with very little real time on our hands.

This morning I have been sorting through dramatic photographs that came out of artist Jill Cater's 'museum of possibilities' and inspired my new magazine 'Domestic Cherry' under the editorship of Mabel Watson, my alter ego. Mabel is a woman ten years older, much wiser and perhaps more daring than I and she creates a kind of theatrical playfulness in this literature exploit. I hope to engage women writers and artists in something serious but slightly fantastical; challenging the stuffiness that seems to come with highbrow publications (excuse me, just a minute; while I reload the washing machine and butter a cracker for William as he must have it now!). That's not to say that I will be publishing poetry and art that isn't in my own understanding brilliant; no, that's the point. I believe women with a playful experimental nature make the best artists and poets and will therefore be drawn to Mrs Watson's feather boa and pakka mac. I am seeking work of humuor, honesty and loaded with it's own love of the medium. Above all I am looking for the fresh, quirky, amazing or the deeply moving. I am not always looking for polished because sometimes a poem comes along and says something strange like "I am attending to enjoyment" because of the language it was translated from isn't English and reminds me yes, I should attend to my own enjoyment, more often.

This week I am working in prison, inspiring the men there to love poetry too. And I say love because I could go along with sheets of paper directing them in what it takes to create a poem but I have come to the conclusion that before anyone desires to write it, they must love it first. And from the enthusiasm of the last session I think I might be half way there. I was invited after the session to visit one of the warden's 15 year old boys "can you possibly do the same for my son?" Love is infectious and sells like hotcakes (another cliche but when you're busy...)

I am also practicing with my fellow BlueGate Poets our performance of Valerie Clark poems at Bath Literature Festival on February 25th. Sadly Valerie died before she could hold her wonderful book in her hands and perform them herself. We are doing this great honor for her.

This is a short snippet of the kind of chaos my love for poetry brings to my life. When I should be cleaning I'm usually writing a poem, when I should be making beds I'm daydreaming the next poem and when I should be organising I'm usually discussing the next great project. Hmm, what will become of me? Will I drown in my own washing basket before my first book, if I am so lucky, floats up to the great heights of a shelf in Waterstones wearing a life jacket?

Mum's the word

MUM'S THE WORD

Thanks to Liz Brackenbury for this great critique of what is a mum

Position available: Mum

Experience: None required.

Training: On-the-job training provided free for the duration of the contract.

Length of contract: Life

Hours of work: 24 hours a day, 7 days a week, 52 Weeks of the year, year after year after…

Pay: Yes, with your sanity!

Essential requirements: Broad shoulders, a big heart and even bigger bank balance.

Job description: A challenging but varied position awaits the right candidate. Must have the ability to think on your feet (well there's little chance of sitting down!) and be flexible (emotionally and bodily!) Can work effectively in a highly pressured and chaotic environment and perform resourcefully as part of a team and individually using own initiative. Most work will however be on your own even though you are part of a team, (when it's them verses you – trust me your on your own!) Must possess the ability to communicate efficiently in demanding and awkward situations. Candidates should have the organizational skills of the army plus hold a Black Cab knowledge of local area as the ability to drive short distances within unachievable timescales is essential. A degree in cake baking and costume design would be preferable, as your role will involve making fancy dress outfits with a 12 hour turn around and producing cakes to rival Mr Kipling for fundraising events. Experience with circus skills would prove a useful addition to your portfolio as you will find yourself juggling a million things at once. A vital requirement is to be prepared for the unpreparable.

Job duties: Be responsible at all times (even when irresponsibility seems a better option). Provide 24 hour unconditional support and a full back up service all year round plus offer extra support both emotional and financial as and when required (and it will be, often!). To honor the responsibility to be resourceful, resilient and run ragged. Also to have the patience of a saint, the morals of a judge, the skin of a rhino, the memory of an elephant, the energy an energetic thing, the speed of light and more balls than a bingo caller. In addition you must remain cool, calm, collected, conscientious, centred, creative, clever, clean, and… sorry I got carried away … I meant 'whilst remaining sane!' Overtime mandatory!

Additional skills: To fulfill the role effectively it is beneficial to have some experience in being a home maker, a taxi service, a counsellor, entertainer, medic, psychologist, therapist, any other form of career ending in *-ist, -gist* or *-pist* (wine helps) is favorable. A military background in discipline and crowd control (for when their friends come for tea) would be helpful as would a CRSR check (Child Ready Surely being a mum can't be that hard Reality check).

Application deadline: Changes month to month.

Benefits: Varied work load. Loyalty Scheme (subject to change). Job for life! Good luck!

Cristina (Navazo-Eguía) Newton

Spanish-born, now lives in Britain. First published two full-length collections — La Frontera and Rutas de Largo Recorrido — and some of my English poems have appeared in journals. Organise the Battered Moon Poetry Competition linked to the Swindon Literature Festival and Artswords. Involved in adult education, wildlife and literary projects, cante hondo and raising my three very lively children.

Daystart

She is set to time even in sleep. Her sleep is that of the wrung-out, a sink-down, blank-out rehearsal of the ultimate rescue. The all-out-sleep of gratefulness. Time just slides down in her sleep, she's in Good-Father's inglenook. She's set to time so no man-made mechanism can touch her sleep. She wakes before noise, beats the alarm of clocks to the here-we-are, the fringe where the body tears with a certain pain from rest. First to mind is whose child she is, whose life, what day of the week, what stage of life, what place on earth, what she will give them for their lunch. What must be done. A day to put history in place and push it on its way. So she puts on her legs, her hands, her working self. Her face is still a blur of dates. She has the franchise to break the morning's shell and start to pour it before the rest awake, so the dark will be a smooth lived-in room with the door left slightly ajar. The body parts have to be transported to the assembly room, where the whole comes of age and everything that has not yet been done casts a little disappointed shadow. Move on, move on, there is this day to be made. How strange to start the day in night. Let her see how the world's got on outside, let her assess the skills of winter, the accomplishments of frost. Creation is on the go, running on hungerpangs; the human race is late. No time to waste when all hangs on one's arms. The wrappings of sleep have to come off. Down to the primordial state of humankind, exposure to electric light and cold. Down to the bare necessities and the screening of age-damaged cells. Let's get rid of the musty taste and smell of the animal life. Water. The clean easy water of the privileged west. The blessing of tapped heat. The warmth and scents of the prepackaged world. Let's start our life again with thanks. That no-one kicked down our front door carrying guns. That no one dragged us from our beds. That no-one has burst into the bathroom while we spent our waste or stood stark naked in this cubicle of rain. That no one has scratched another on the face or sat on someone's neck. That no-one's screams for clean underwear have cracked this private peace. Not yet. If no-one wrestled with this rhythm of silent duties, and things could be done at one's own plain-sailing pace. No word to be said before all the maintainance works are over and done with, and one can speak with liberty in the spirit and in verse.

She's not quite finished drying and they are fisting the bathroom's door, calling loud to be let in, giving her a jumpstart of the heart.

Tracy Smith

A full time working mum. Live in small village.
Member of a small but select great wine group.

Day Diary of a Working Mum

2am   Awake again. Worrying about work, the rising workload, and whether my younger son will settle at school this term or if I should change schools. Lie awake weighing up pros and cons. Worry about making right decision as it could affect my son's future.

Turn radio on. Recently discovered ball by ball cricket commentary, which is normally much more effective than counting sheep. However, thanks to very exciting Ashes test, am now awake cheering England on!

4am   Cat meowing, it has brought me a 'present'. Unfortunately it's still alive and shoots across room, diving under TV cabinet, with cat in hot pursuit. Husband not pleased and muttering "that cat must go".

6am   Dog whining to go out. Dog comes back in, sees cat and hurtles after it. Before I can grab it, it's up the stairs and into the kids' bedrooms.

Thomas (11) now awake and asking for breakfast, which blows any chance of going back to bed.

6–8.30am Usual chaos, nagging kids to eat breakfast, get ready for school etc. They pay their usual attention, ignoring me in favour of the TV. Feed rabbit, two cats, dog, hamster (only one now thanks to cat), three fish. Finally ready to leave house, but dog (Jack Russell) senses this and makes bid for freedom through cat flap (another reason my husband hates cats). I'm wearing high heels so send my kids into farmyard to catch dog, who has gone hunting at back of nearby cowshed. Their shoes smell nice when they get back in car! We're late for school again.

Indulge myself on drive to work by turning up the music and singing along "Oh oh, living on a prayer…"

Huff and puff my way up five flights of stairs to where my office is located, telling myself for the millionth time that I really must lose weight.

Open up office, to register my presence, and then sneak off to canteen with two colleagues for our Friday treat of bacon rolls and a cappuccino. It's then a busy day for me in my role as Trademark paralegal for a large electronics company.

2.30pm   Time to turn into a Mum again. Down tools for dash to playground.

3.05pm   Pouring with rain. Drive along wondering why it always rains when the kids are coming out of school and I haven't brought a coat. Boys unhappy that I'm late again.

William (8) can't wait to tell me that there will be no swimming this term, due to a fire at the sports centre. Drive to local town. Can't park; circle the car park three times before getting a space. Maybe it's my lucky day after all, bought new daps and school shoes, both in the sales and at the final reductions. I love a bargain.

5pm   I hear "What's for tea" and "Why isn't it ready yet?" from the boys. My creative powers are used up for the day so it's spaghetti bolognaise with sauce from a jar.

7.30–9pm Husband returns; bedtime routines; and finally, after arguments about what constitutes appropriate weekend bedtime, peace at last.

10pm   Desert my husband and go to bed with a book. Can hear gnawing sounds in the corner of the room. Don't think cat caught the mouse again. Hope my husband doesn't notice.

Sue Webster

34, married with three children — four, three and one years.
Run own on-line business in partnership with sister.

Getting Going

Oh it can't be that time already, surely? It is still dark. Someone obviously thinks it is morning by the sound of it. I reach over and grab my mobile to see the time, squinting at the bright light on the display. Aaargh… it is 7.40 already. Thank goodness the baby woke me up. Time to get going or we'll be late!

Every day I say to myself that I will be more organised and set my alarm. At least be up and dressed first. Maybe even make a cup of tea to get me going. But the temptation of that extra five minutes of sleep when you've been up in the night with one or more of them is always too strong. So, as usual, the baby already has a head start on me, demanding to be picked up, nappy changed and fed and I still can't even open my eyes properly yet! Probably when I am halfway through one of those things another one will wake up and start calling for me, so back up the stairs I'll go. But I will have to carry the baby with me otherwise he'll get all upset and start crying, so it's back up the stairs we go together. And back down I come with one on each hip, closely followed by a sleepy boy.

I never go to the gym these days. Don't have the time. But then I don't think I need to, all this running around after three little ones and carrying one or more of them certainly keeps me fit. I start wondering to myself how long it will be until they are old enough to make me breakfast? Even bring it to me in bed… now that would be nice…

Enough of the daydreaming, it is now 7.55 and there are three little ones to feed, get dressed and out of the door (and one shoe is bound to be missing). Not forgetting myself of course… I still haven't had a chance to get dressed yet and it would be terribly embarrassing to turn up at school in my pyjamas and slippers. I am surprised it hasn't happened yet to be honest! I doubt I will have time for the breakfast bit. Will just grab that burnt crust of toast that one of them has left. That will keep me going for now.

8.45 and finally we are ready to leave the house. Why is it that no matter what time we get up we always seem to be rushing out of the door at quarter to nine? As we step outside I realise it is the first time I have actually looked outside this morning. I hadn't seen that there had been a hard frost and the car is covered in ice. Great. The quickest thing would be to go back in and get some warm water for the windscreen but no, now I have finally managed to get all three of them out here I am not going back in. First things first, get these three in the car and strapped in before they escape, off to do something more interesting.

This is the hardest part of the whole morning. How can an 8 month old be so strong in resisting sitting down in his car seat? It seems there is no way his body is going to bend in the middle. There. Finally. He's in. Right, now for the other two. I am sure it must have been easier in the days when you could just bundle all the kids in the back and off you go. Now the hunt for something to scrape the ice off the windscreen. It is ten to nine now. Why can't I be more organised? It is a good job the school is only just over a mile away. Tina Turner CD case, that will do the trick.

Running into school, quick, quick, we mustn't be late for the register. "But where's my book bag Mum?" Back to the car we go.

"Quick, in you go". "Ten kisses and a big hard cuddle Mum". I give him the ten kisses, plus a bonus one and a squeeze and in he goes with a big smile.

That's it… I feel I have already done a day… and it is only 9am (well, 2 minutes past…we were almost on time).

Cath Kimmins

36 years old, Mum of two, wife of one. Am very family orientated, love new challenges and pressure and like to keep busy most of the time. Think I am a 'people person', a good listener and friend. I worry far too much about what others think of me and can be quite emotional, but I put this down to my genes! Love going out for meals and enjoying a bottle of good wine with friends.

Just Another Day

My children attend the local infant school and although they enjoy school and have lots of friends, getting them ready and out of the door before the school bell rings can be quite stressful!

My day starts about 7am when we are generally woken by Ben who is always starving hungry! Rosie takes a while to wake up and generally needs a bit of a cuddle before she can even consider being nice to anyone! The children have breakfast and then are ushered back upstairs to brush their teeth and hair and get dressed. If we have time, they like to play a game but I generally try and get on one load of washing before leaving the house and like to clean up the breakfast things. I try and walk my children to school as often as I can. This can take up to 30 minutes depending if we are doing a 'slow' walk up the steep hill. Children of this age have no sense of urgency unless it is something they want to do. I often end up raising my voice and threatening all sorts of things in desperation to get them to hurry up! If the weather is bad though, I have to admit I relent and will drive.

The rest of the day is spent on household chores and preparing a healthy tea that the children will enjoy. Tim will eat anything, so he is no trouble at all! I also run my own small business so I am constantly worrying about how to make it more successful and get more sales. Two afternoons a week I also volunteer in the school. I thoroughly enjoy this and I get to see my children in a different environment. This also allows me to see what they actually do at school as when I ask them they can never remember!

I return to school for 3pm to pick the children up. This is a good time to have a quick chat with the other mums in the playground. Ben and Rosie are always 'starving' when they come out, so, if we are walking home then I will bring them a snack. 3 out of 5 days of the school week, one of them has an after school class – ballet, football, Beavers. Depending on the time of the class depends on when they have their tea but we try and sit down as a family for tea at least twice a week and then at the weekends.

The rest of the afternoon is a general battle to get them to do their reading homework and spellings. I am always trying to come up with a fun idea to get them to do it but generally it does result in bribery!

Tim returns from work at about 6pm. They then spend some time with him before having a bath. Tim will generally do the bedtime stories whilst I clean up after tea, make the packed lunches for the next day, sort out school uniforms… etc etc!

I finally sit down and relax after about 9pm but I would not have it any other way!

Karen Smith

Live in Wiltshire. Married mother of two: Harry aged four and Matilda twenty months. Ex-customer relations administrator, now have discovered what real tiredness is! Also discovering a passion for writing!

Where Did I Go?

Where did I go?
Just for a minute, I want to know
Set adrift on a sea of unknown
Surrounded by toys, no time alone…
Some times are good, some times bad
Days it comes together and days of going mad!
The smiles are worth it, of that I'm sure
The tears however, push me a little more…
Sometimes I feel like I'm watching through glass
Remembering the old me and adventures from the past
I know things will change soon enough
I worry that all I'll remember is times that were tough
I scream sometimes and cry myself to sleep
For my little children can make me weep…
They bring me laughter too
So for this, I'll keep on working through…
I lose myself in Heat and Hello! Magazine
But don't worry, the kitchen's clean
Dinner on the table and music groups done
Swimming lessons, softplay and all that fun!
Where did I go?
One day I know I will know…
Two lives formed with lives of their own…
Time for me at last! Now pass the phone

Naomi Whitehouse

Thirty-six year old mother of nine, married for 15 years. Born in Rotterdam to an English father and Dutch mother. I enjoyed writing from an early age and wrote many poems as a teenager, mainly as therapy for my own thoughts and feelings. I completed two years of my degree in French and German at Bradford Uni before leaving to care for our first daughter Bethany. Being a mother has brought me fulfilment, but that's not to say it isn't challenging at times!

Just a Mum!

The Paradoxical 'Just A Mum'
I work every minute, day and night
In my new role
My sleep, my meals and daydreams
Are no longer all my own.
My new role is:
'Just a mum'.
I belong to the mass of unbeknowns,
Now 'Tomorrow's World' is in my arms.
While those who work their nine-to-five
Are paid and hold their heads high.
No money received, no honours conferred
For the most precious workload on earth.
'Just a Mum' is the title.
The challenge a big game
Yet 'In The Balance' lies
Whether our world will stay the same.
Our decisions must be swift and sure
Our heart remain engaged.
The glistening sunshine is our wage
The joy in our baby's eye.
The heart's warmth no money can provide
Many consolations, our pride;
The Wonder
Of unfolding human life.

Louise Finlayson

I practised as a corporate finance lawyer in London for many years before moving to Scotland with my husband. I am now enjoying having the opportunity to spend some time being a full-time mum.

A Mother's Instinct

It was three days after my emergency c-section. Although I was still in hospital and desperately trying to cling to the final vestiges of dignity, I was quite honestly the most excited new mummy in the world. I really wish I could put down in words how I felt in those first few days but there are no feelings that come close to describing the heady mix of love, sheer excitement and pure exhaustion. A cocktail of emotions that really bring you to the brink of delirium!

I did not have any pre-conceived ideas about what life would be like after the birth of my baby but I was firm that I wanted to breast feed, rather than bottle feed, if at all possible because I believed this would give him the best start in life.

For those first three days I thought I had cracked it. I very diligently ensured that my son had his first feed soon after birth and then seemed to feed him continually. In reality, however, it was only every few hours, day and night. It was such a labour of love but I did not mind. I was acutely aware that this tiny, squidgey bundle relied on me for everything and I would do anything for him.

Day three is critical because it is the day on which your newborn is weighed and a decision is made as to whether your feeding regime is working. When the midwife weighed my son I was shocked to learn that he had apparently lost more than the permitted ten per cent of his birth weight and I would need to give him some formula milk straight away. I was distraught. On the one hand I felt such despair that he had lost so much weight and on the other I could not reconcile what they were telling me with what I perceived the reality to be: that he was gaining weight – he seemed heavier and I felt that I had a lot of milk to give him.

As the midwife stood beside me and prepared to open the bottle of formula milk the exhaustion and frustration overwhelmed me. It was ridiculous really. I had no issue with the principle of giving a baby formula. My issue lay with the fact that I felt I did not have to. I knew he was eating, not only could I feel it but I could also see it.

Aware of my despair the well-meaning but slightly fierce midwife gave me a reprieve of an hour during which time I had to express my milk into a bottle. If I succeeded in expressing the required amount in that time she told me that she would be happy for us to re-assess the situation and reconsider the options. It took me five minutes to express the requisite amount. An hour later I had enough for a week. I felt like I had won the lottery, triumph quickly trumping the day's earlier feelings of anger and frustration, which soon felt like distant memories.

Then began the long process of syringing minute amounts into him. We got there though and I feel so lucky that I was able to persevere. It was definitely the right thing for me to do and was a real lesson in trusting your instincts when it comes to knowing what is best for you and your baby.

I can now look back on that day positively, from despair to elation. I am still utterly besotted with my baby and I continually watch him in wonder and think how much we have both learned in the past twelve months.

Rebecca Doyle

32, married, and very happy mother of two year-old twins, living in Tunbridge Wells.

A Mother's Nightmare

April 24th 2010 started like any other Saturday in our house. We had a family breakfast together, and it was the usual mad-house with our 18-month-old twins!

My husband was in the garden putting our new barbeque together with our twin-son Max, whilst I took Isabella, our twin-daughter, out shopping. We had a lovely time together.

It was a beautiful sunny day so after shopping, we went and joined the boys in the garden. At around midday, Isabella started screaming in a high-pitched manner and was rubbing her head. We assumed she'd bumped her head on the slide but after a few moments, she calmed down and we thought nothing more of it. We had lunch in the garden and I put Max and Isabella down for their nap.

When I went to pick Isabella up out of her cot after her nap, her arms were limp and floppy and she had a temperature of 39°C. She was breathing very quickly and gasping. I phoned our out-of-hours doctors and they said they would get a doctor to phone back within the hour.

By 3.30pm Isabella was just slumped on the sofa staring into space. I knew something wasn't right and felt a knot form in my stomach. I can only describe it as a real moment of instinct and I knew I had to get a doctor to see her quickly. I put Isabella in the car and drove to A&E. My husband stayed at home with Max.

We were taken to a cubicle and a nurse came to do Isabella's observations. He hooked her up to a heart monitor we could see her heart was racing, her pulse was through the roof and her temperature had soared to 39.9°C. A rash had appeared on Isabella's chest, face, back and neck. She was losing consciousness and wouldn't respond to me calling her name. I felt sick with fear.

Within minutes our cubicle was filled with doctors and nurses. There were tubes being put into both of Isabella's feet and hands. She was hooked up to three intravenous drips and she had an oxygen mask on. The x-ray team were taking chest x-rays and other nurses were taking blood samples from her feet. The Consultant confirmed my worst fears and said he thought that Isabella had meningitis. Everything was happening so quickly, my husband was at home with Max and I hadn't even had the chance to call him to tell him what was going on.

Isabella was given a huge dose of antibiotics and the Consultant came back to speak to me. Isabella was unconscious by that stage and he told me to prepare for the worst. There were two ambulances outside waiting to take us to St Thomas' Hospital in London. The Consultant said the next 24 hours would be critical. Isabella would have to be put into a medically-induced coma to prevent her lungs from collapsing. I just kept thinking what if she doesn't wake up.

We were taken into theatre. It was so surreal. My worst nightmare had come true. How could this be happening? The Consultant told me I had to get my husband to come in and be with us both. We don't have family nearby so a friend came over to look after Max.

At 7pm my husband arrived at A&E and the most miraculous thing happened. Isabella's rash had started to subside and she was coming round. As my husband walked into theatre, Isabella said "Dada". It was just incredible. It was a new beginning for us all. Whilst still very poorly, Isabella had come through the worst of it. Once she was stable enough we were transported by ambulance to the paediatric ward at Pembury Hospital. The next few days and weeks were horrendously worrying and tough. Max was brought in to hospital and also treated for meningitis as he was showing symptoms of the illness.

We are so lucky that Isabella and Max have both made a full recovery. A lot of children aren't as lucky. If you do one thing today, read and learn the symptoms of this terrifying illness.

Lauren Reynolds

Born Swindon 1972, grew up in Wiltshire, UK. Left school had variety of jobs before working for an Environmental Research Company who still employ me twenty years on! After my first yoga class, I loved it so much I decided to train to be a teacher Qualified November 2002. Married to a fireman, have three-year-old twin boys; am a huge animal lover, vegan and am actively involved in fund raising for animal charities. I would like to be thought of as a compassionate, ethical, person devoted to my family and loyal to my friends.

Parenting the Yoga Way

In yoga philosophy there are ten traditional Yamas, the 'ethical rules' or Yoga's Ten Commandments. I try to live in accordance with these as best I can. However, I'm no guru, and I often fail!

The Yamas are:

Ahimsa: Nonviolence. Abstinence from injury; harmlessness, the not causing of pain to any living creature in thought, word, or deed at any time.

Satya: truthfulness, word and thought in conformity with the facts.

Asteya: non-stealing, non-coveting, non-entering into debt.

Brahmacharya: divine conduct, continence, celibate when single, faithful when married.

Kshama: patience, releasing time, functioning in the now.

Dhriti: steadfastness, overcoming non-perseverance, fear, and indecision; seeing each task through to completion.

Daya: compassion; conquering callous, cruel and insensitive feelings toward all beings.

Arjava: honesty, straightforwardness, renouncing deception and wrongdoing.

Mitahara: moderate appetite, neither eating too much nor too little: not consuming meat, fish, shellfish, fowl or eggs.

Shaucha: purity, avoidance of impurity in body, mind and speech

My students probably think my day begins and ends with me sat cross legged in lotus position in a tranquil Zen garden meditating on the sounds of nature. The reality is very different. As a working mother of three-year-old twin boys and various fur/feather babies, my household is more mad than mellow! Day begins at 6am. I tiptoe around hoping that the boys don't hear me and I can get ready in peace but invariably, their owl-like sense of hearing locates my whereabouts and they're stood beside me saying "I need a wee wee".

All parent know that it's an unwritten rule that your child's needs come before you own, so before I can have that 'I-can't-function-until-I've-had-my-first-cup-of-tea', it's milk and toast for the kids. Now it's light outside the chickens are squawking from their coop demanding to be let out, so the next job is to trudge out in my dressing gown and wellies to feed and water them and the guinea pigs hoping that the neighbours don't see this dishevelled, unglamorous me! Then it's the dog's turn to be served.

Finally, the boys are entertaining themselves, and I can make my cup of tea and get ready, until a wail from the other room indicates they're fighting. This is where I practice 'Kshama' (patience). One of the many things that yoga has taught me is learning when to push and when to surrender. I'm still working on when to let go in my mothering life.

On a non-office day we go for a walk with the dog. Previously this was a calm, care-free experience that required nothing more than grabbing a collar, lead and poop bag as we're heading out the door. Now leaving the house requires military precision as the boys try every trick in the book to avoid putting on their shoes or coats. The park is full of distractions – other dogs, swings incredibly appealing even though they're soaking wet, and worms who HAVE to be studied to decide whether it's a 'mummy' or 'daddy' worm. This is an opportunity to teach the boys 'Ahimsa' (non-violence). I think it's important to instil compassion and respect for all living beings into a child's life in the hope that they'll grow up to be kind and caring adults.

Back home and I unroll my yoga mat. I've barely stepped on it before the kids are climbing all over me and the dog is sniffing my ear. So after I've sneaked just one pose in, the mat goes away.

Shopping! I do my best to include the boys asking them whether they want strawberries or bananas, pasta or fish fingers. Most times it keeps them happy but some days the chaos begins the minute we walk through the door and it's so embarrassing when they collapse a display and "Clean up on aisle two" blares from the speakers.

Home, lunch, then, thankfully, nap time. I now have two hours to do – a little housework, cleaning out the animals and a couple more yoga poses. Even in a couple of minutes I can focus on my breath or stand in Tree Pose whilst washing up. Just because time is restricted, doesn't mean I can't stand on one leg!

Occasionally we visit a soft play area where 'Daya' (conquering insensitive feelings toward all beings) gets challenged. It always irks me when parents leave their children unsupervised at a public play area and then refuse to accept any responsibility when their child hurts another in some way, but it's not the 'little monsters' that test my 'Daya', it's the parents!

Once home, it's dinner, bath and bedtime. One of the boys is the slowest eater in the world at dinner-time and, since I need to get them to bed before my yoga class, it would be easier to let him leave half his food. Instead I practice both 'Kshama' (patience) and 'Dhriti' (seeing a task through to completion) so, as agonizingly frustrating as it is, I persevere.

Class over, back home I'm trying to practice 'Mitahara' (neither eating too much nor too little). Sometimes I am so exhausted, I just want to bath and fall into bed totally bypassing food altogether. Other times I am so famished that I will literally raid the fridge like a woman possessed. Either way, I love bedtime. I LOVE going to sleep. Benjamin Franklin said "Fatigue is the best pillow" and after a typical day, that pillow could not be any more inviting.

Liz Brackenbury

Freelance writer. Live in Swindon, Wiltshire. Mum of seven – five boys and two girls and, at the most intense, had six under the age of eight years. 'Fell' into writing a column for the local paper with no previous writing experience. My colourful and vibrant family life inspires and gives me plenty of new ideas on a daily basis!

Who's Yummy?

Yummy Mummy? What a pretentious misconception of motherhood! It used to be normal to expect new mums to be tired, out of shape, 'out of action'and live in pyjamas for months. I don't mean in a slummy mummy way, but just in a realistic kind of one. Most of us used to look forward to the rest after nine months of pregnancy and childbirth!

Yummy Mummy! The high profile celebrity culture of women who parade their flawless bodies, expensive lifestyles and beautifully groomed children in front of the camera making motherhood seem the most effortless and glamorous of undertakings. They just forget, however to mention the army of staff, personal trainers and money it takes behind the scenes to achieve this false pretence of perfection! Their lifestyles are unrealistic and unachievable even for them to maintain single handedly so why is it that today's mums are aiming to attain the impossible?

Yummy Mummy, the super sexy, super clever, career driven, super mum. Its an image created by women but why? Even men don't get it! Women really can be their own worst enemies. Yummy Mummies have become the idealistic benchmark that women *can* have it all, when in reality we all know it is women who end up *doing* it all!

Being a mum is hard work, giving this absurd impression that life is perfect is enough to have any normal person reaching for the prozac!

Back in reality-land can you honestly imagine Posh 'n' Becks pairing up socks for an evening's entertainment They've probably got a sock nanny or maybe designer socks that stick together dahlings. All I know is that my cheapy socks are all now single. Maybe I could start a speed dating for socks, you know, spots or stripes, blue or red, perfect match or back to singlesocksville! 7 children x 7 days of the week thats 49 pairs of socks per week And I can't find a single pair! Opinion is divided in my house. The girls think it's the sock fairy that steals all the socks to make a home in the base of the sofa along with all the coins, hairgrips, pens and fluff to re-house all the orphan fairies who failed the tooth fairy test versus the boys who think it's the mischievous sock monster that lives in the washing machine and steals them to make more sock monsters that will take over the universe! I've tried everything, bright stripy, spotty even neon ones, and still not one pair in sight, I am a sock mum failure! Maybe we should all chill out and start a miss-match sock rebellion, even yummy mummies might find it fashionable too!

Monica Timms

Born Chichester, moved to Swindon in 1974 for my husband's job. I have three children and two grandchildren and four step-grandchildren. Have always been a compulsive writer although not great at finishing pieces. Have kept a journal since the 1980s. Love walking and reading. This house is full of books. I need books around me to read otherwise I get withdrawal symptoms

Thoughts on Being a Parent to Adult Children

It's 8.30 in the evening and the telephone rings. We look at each other. Which one will it be, and what will they want? The husband goes to answer it.

"Hello Toots"
I hear him say… so it's the daughter.
If he says
"Hello vicar"
It's a son.

I hear snatches of conversation, laughter, the grandsons' names mentioned.
Eventually I hear him say:
"Do you want to speak to your Mother?"
She obviously says "Yes" because he appears in the doorway, beckoning me.
"Here she comes" he tells her.

"Hello Sweetie"
I say
"How are you?"

I ask about the grandsons and son-in-law and she tells me what they've been up to.
Just when I think it might be time to say goodbye she says
"Oh, by the way, what are you doing…?"

We know what is coming – a request to baby-sit usually
or
"Can we come and visit you?"
which means Nanna cooks lunch and makes cakes for tea.
or
"Can you come to tea"
which also means "can Nanna make come cakes?"
or
"Can we borrow…"

When the daughter left home and borrowed any of our equipment we bought that item for her for Christmas, in the hope that we could have ours back.

I have suggested to the husband that he create a spreadsheet to show which child has which piece of equipment, tool, or whatever they've borrowed, so that when we go to the cupboard or drawer to look for something and it's not there we will know who has it and "can we please borrow it back!"

Susan Cook

Essex girl, born Rochford 1953. Moved to the West Country in 2000 in preparation for my husband's retirement. Hobbies: reading, cooking, photography and travel. Volunteer at local Day Centre and friend of a residential care home.

Alternative Motherhood

When people think of the word motherhood it is usually associated with bringing up children. Although I had always wanted children – it never happened. I slowly became a carer for my mum-in-law Marge who at the time was living with us and in a strange way I took over the role of her mother. It was a completely different way of life from what I had been used to, working full time since I was seventeen and culminating my career in my early fifties as secretary P.A. to a managing director after which we moved to the south west.

A major difference I believe between motherhood and looking after an elderly parent is you have 9 months knowing you are eventually going to become a parent but sometimes you just slowly drift into caring and on reflection you have quite a shock as to how much your life has changed without actually realising it at the time.

Caring for Marge was at times exasperating, time consuming and tiring (both mentally and physically) but this was all vastly outweighed by the love and good times we had together. These are the memories which are treasured and everything else fades into insignificance. At odd times she would put her head on my shoulder and whisper "love you" and give me a big hug not seeming to want to let go. At these times your heart melted.

Going from being a somewhat deep sleeper I now slept with one ear focused on any noise coming from Marge's bedroom. I would be out of bed like a rocket and into her room, usually to find she was rearranging her clothes in her wardrobe or perhaps astounded at how her bedroom furniture had arrived. Each morning would begin with her usual call of my name following by "cooeee" and if I didn't arrive quick enough clothes would be put on in a somewhat haphazard order. Getting ready in the morning was never a quick process but when the person you are caring for is in her late 80s being in a rush is impossible. We had our fun times, one being on taking Marge shopping and loading up her wheelchair with packages (you could hardly see her under the various parcels).

My 'first day at school' experience came on the day that Marge first went to a day care centre. We had been advised to take her in an hour late so everyone would be settled and she could meet everybody more easily. The big day came and we walked into the centre hand-in-hand hoping that all was going to be well and she was going to settle. We didn't want to leave her (it must be like leaving your five year old on their first day at school) and on closing the door behind us I promptly burst into tears wondering whether she was going to be alright. Every hour on the hour I said to my husband "I wonder what Marge is doing now, hoped she liked the lunch and everyone is nice to her". We couldn't hold out until the end of the day and went into collect her about an hour early – just in case. She couldn't have been happier and came out of the centre proudly showing off a painting she had done that afternoon. I had visions of paintings and sketches pinned all over the kitchen walls but we managed to keep them to a bare minimum, changing old ones for new when the time came.

Sadly Marge had to eventually go into full time residential care but we visited her almost every day but the role reversals were still there. When she called out for 'Mummy' she meant her own mum but when she asked for 'Mum' she meant me.

She was a grand little lady and I can honestly say her illness and my looking after her helped me lay some of the ghosts I had in not having children of my own and I am proud that for a few years I was her 'mum'.

I love what I'm doing

I LOVE WHAT I'M DOING

Lena Doherty

Mummy to four and wifey to one. Self employed Virtual Assistant with own VA and Media Company called Freelance Media. Also a part-time Celebrity and Entertainments writer for an online mag/blog called Brew Drinking Thinkings.

Am I Lucky?

I consider myself to be one of the lucky ones. Not having to commute to work every day, no traffic jams, no office politics, no boss to scream and shout at me. Someone asked me a few days ago what I love the most about working from home.

I didn't have to even think about it, I had a million and one things running around my head so here are my top 10 things I love about working from home:

In the summer I can take my laptop out into the garden and work. Not only is this beneficial to my own well being, but I can think back to those days when I worked in stuffy offices with no air conditioning. I can also have a sneaky ice lolly because no one is watching me (well except for that dodgy neighbour).

I no longer have to worry about the washing, if it's sunny I can step away from my desk and put the washing out and if it starts to rain I can step away from my desk and bring it back in.

I never get to work and think "Shit, I forgot to put the bin out" or "Crap, I forgot my lunch".

I can work wherever I want to. In the conservatory, in the kitchen, in the garden or even in Asda! Yep that's right folks with the art of modern technology I have the ability to answer emails, even when I'm doing my weekly shop.

Distractions, there are hundreds of them every day in the office. At home I have none, well apart from Little Monster but he is a welcome distraction. I don't have to get caught up in the office bitch fest and I certainly don't have to worry about getting caught by the office creep!

Childcare fees, these were the bane of my life. I seemed to be working just to pay these, no more! I can do both school runs and be there in the holidays. Even when the school calls to say Little Princess is sick I can go without the worry of a boss breathing down my neck.

A little siesta, these were never possible in the office and only ever possible now if Monster is poorly as he never sleeps in the day. But just to curl up on the sofa and have a ten minute power nap, wow it really does work.

Office wardrobe, in the office these consisted of either a smart uniform or a simple dress code. Not on my watch my office dress code is anything from PJ's, hoodies and jeans, or baggy jumpers and leggings and maybe the odd pair of tracksuit pants. Unless I'm meeting with a client or networking then it's back to smart and sensible.

Working whenever I want to. I suffer from insomnia from time to time, so I will put this time to good use by finishing clients files, sorting out my own paperwork or even doing a bit of blogging.

The greatest thing about working from home is the freedom. I can eat and drink at my desk, I can talk to my sister on the phone, I can work from the local coffee shop if I need some fresh air, I can be as creative as I want to be with my work and no one will tell me I can't do it, I can nip to the park for a game of footie with Monster as long as I have my phone with me for important emails, I can do whatever I want and I LOVE IT.

So that's it, all those things above are all the things I love because I am extremely lucky enough to be able to work from home. There are downsides, but the ups outweigh the down.

I have always wanted to be able to work from home, we could never afford for me to be a SAHM, so I had to work for the sake of my family, but now I do, and I love what I do.

Lesley Soane

51, married to Tony for four years, three grandchildren with another due in July. Swindon born and bred, Project Manager for Network Rail. Favourite things — family and friends getting together at our house, having the grandchildren for sleepovers, the challenge of answering "Nanny what, why, how...?" and sometimes not knowing how to answer. Proudest achievement — bringing up a beautiful daughter practically on my own and watching her blossom into a wonderful young mum and wife.

Addicted Baker

It is true. I have to face the fact that I am living with an addiction and it has taken over my spare time... I am addicted to baking! I would like to explain how this began...

In 2005 my daughter was expecting her first baby. She experienced some complications half way through the pregnancy which worried us all. I found myself unable to settle in the

evenings so searched for something that would distract me from the constant worrying, so turned to baking! An unusual choice for me as I had not baked since my school days. I worked full time in a managerial role and so felt tired after a busy day in the office but this still didn't quell my urge to bake. I started off baking fairly simple things like plain scones and fairy cakes and instantly found it very therapeutic and calming. I loved the aroma of baking which filled the house (a bit like that lovely homely feeling you get when you are in the supermarket and you can smell the freshly baked bread) and it conjured up memories of my childhood. The sense of pride I felt when I took out the finished items from the oven was great!

You must be thinking what on earth did she do with all those cakes well, fortunately I worked with a 'captive' audience at work so had forty willing guinea pigs, oops I mean recipients there, shared them with friends and my husband used to take them to his office and share them there too!

Some six years later and I'm still baking most evenings! I am now 'known' as 'the lady who bakes cakes'. I've changed jobs working full time in project management for another large organisation and now my new team thoroughly enjoy the endless array of cakes and biscuits I take in to work to share. One of the first things our grandchildren do when they visit is rush to the kitchen to see what delights are in the stack of cakes tins. My husband has the responsibility of being the 'official taster' and is eager to help out by trying new recipes. Lucky for him he has a good metabolism so has somehow managed to keep control of his weight.

If I hear of someone who is a bit down in the dumps, about to celebrate a birthday or has a special occasion looming I love to surprise them by rustling up a cake or a tin of biscuits. I have been known to leave 'surprise' parcels of baked goodies on doorsteps.

I have tried to cut back on the baking and find something else which brings me as much pleasure but as yet haven't found a replacement. I think home baking is a lovely way to show someone you've been thinking of them let's face it they always taste so much better than shop bought!

I hope you've enjoyed reading my story and, who knows, you may even feel the urge now to dig out the rolling pin or whisk and rustle up something yourself.

I'm sure you will enjoy it and others will too.

Sandy Moore & Pat Leppard

OAP residents of Highworth, Wiltshire.

Thursday Afternoons at the Lions Shop

Let me introduce myself – my name is Sandy Moore. I work as a volunteer with Pat Leppard at the Lions Community Shop in Highworth, near Swindon Wiltshire. We are known as the 'Thursday Girls – Afternoon Session' – the word 'Girls' being very loose indeed as we are both retired ladies. We are part of a team of ten volunteers who cover this charity shop each week. There are no paid managers – all money made goes back into the charity.

Lions Clubs International is the world's largest service club organisation with a network of over 1.3 million men and women with over 44,000 clubs in over 200 countries to answer the needs that challenge communities around the world.

A typical Thursday for Pat starts early morning, walking her two King Charles Spaniels, doing her housework and making sure her evening meal is ready for when she gets home. I also get my evening meal ready during the morning and luckily for me, my husband Ray helps me with the housework.

We both arrive at the shop for a 1pm start and have a quick look round at anything that may have come in during the week. The Lions Shop sells literally everything and anything from furniture to clothes and shoes. If you want anything out of the ordinary, you don't have to go far to get hold of it – we have trouble sometimes knowing exactly what everything is for!

During the afternoon there is a steady stream of customers coming into the shop. However, there are quite a few things to be done during the afternoon – cleaning the floor, dusting off the furniture and when somebody is moving or has had a good clear out of their house, they bring in lots of articles for us to sell. Sometimes, there can be 10 or 15 bags of clothes and items at one time that need to be sorted and set out on the shelves.

During the year when there are certain festivals such as Christmas and Halloween, we wash and prepare second hand fancy dress outfits which we are able to sell much cheaper – the mums and children don't mind as long as they have something to dress up in. The shop also sells curtains, some of which are in very good condition, but some people come in and need help in measuring up their windows and the different sizes involved.

This shop also serves as an unofficial community centre where people meet up and very often old people come in just for a chat and a sit down with regular customers coming in to just browse around.

At the end of the day we cash up ready for one of the Lions to come in collect and bank the money and if we have had a good afternoon selling items, we feel very pleased with ourselves and go home with a smile on our faces.

Why do we do it? Because we enjoy it!

Emma Blake

Born, bred and lives in Highworth.

Hairdressing

Hello. My name is Emma. I work as a hairdresser and I love my job.

I work in a small local salon in the town where I grew up and still live. One of the reasons I love my job is that it involves meeting interesting and new people and it's never the same two days running. Every client wants something different – colouring, perming, straightening, or cutting. Clients tell me their problems and life stories which I find fascinating.

Hairdressing is known for not being a well paid job. I do it simply for the satisfaction and because I love it. I started training to be a hairdresser in 1989 when I left school. I was placed on a work training scheme (YTS) which meant I went to work in a salon four days a week and college one day a week for a total of two years. As a trainee working in a salon involved meeting and greeting clients, answering the telephone, making appointments, making tea and coffee, cleaning and tidying and generally making sure the salon was presentable.

On my days at college we would have one-and-a-half hours of science, two hours of theory hairdressing and afternoons were spent in the college salon practising on clients that were brave enough to let us loose on their hair under supervision. We also had a 'block' to practice on, which is a plastic head with real hair attached.

After gaining my NVQ (National Vocational Qualification) in hairdressing Levels 1 & 2, I was allowed to work in the salon as a qualified stylist. I continued to work for my first employer for a further eight years and in that time went on to gain a NVQ Level 3 (Business & Management) Level 4 (Avant-Garde and 'Up' styles), Level 5 (NVQ Assessor) which means I can teach and train any apprentices.

I had a break from hairdressing when my first child was young and got a job in the evenings at a local supermarket, but I missed the social side of hairdressing so much I asked a local salon owner on the off-chance if he had any jobs and, luckily, he offered me a part-time position three days-a-week which I took. My hours were gradually increased until I worked full-time.

I have stayed working in the salon and have now worked here for eleven years. Unfortunately the man who first employed me here sadly passed away five years ago. One of my colleagues at the time took over ownership of the salon and decided to keep me on.

We have some really great clients who have a great sense of humour so most days are filled with lots of laughter. On a Friday we have a couple of older clients who come in to share their rude jokes with us. Obviously there are the sadder times when clients move away or die.

I guess I love my job because it's different every day, I work with lovely people and have great clients. I love it.

Juliet Platt

From Lancashire now living in Wiltshire. 'Juggling Mum' freelance writer, run own communication business.

My life is Mad

I have a husband, two children, a hamster and some tropical fish. When the children are at school I run a writing and coaching business; work as a freelance journalist; and organise, promote and run journal-writing and personal development workshops. Sometimes I travel, and rely on my husband to look after the children. Sometimes my mum helps me out.

In my leisure time I write short stories and non-fiction; lead a writers' group; contribute to a philosophy society; read books and talk about them at a book club; play golf and cycle around the place instead of taking the car. Not to mention cheering on my kids in their drama/keyboard/rugby; cooking; washing; ironing; helping with homework and being generally 'around' for them. Thank goodness I have a lady who comes in and does the cleaning for me once a week – that's one less thing on my mind.

Working mothers the whole world over know the juggling that needs to happen in order to do a job, feed the family, keep the house, wash the clothes, get the shopping in. Sometimes I wonder if it's really me getting through all these things. Sometimes I wonder how I manage it.

My life is mad, and I love it.

Every plate I'm spinning – my work, my children, my obsession with reading, writing, learning, debating, golfing, cycling – is piled high with delicious goodies. Every ball I'm keeping up in the air has been especially selected to make me want to play.

It has not always been this way. A few years ago I was trying desperately hard to get my life-coaching business off the ground. Cold-calling, marketing, networking, talking endlessly to people, offering sample sessions, trying to close deals and get new clients in the pipeline – the whole weary process was proving more and more exhausting and less and less what I wanted to do.

So I stopped. I took a ride on my bike and asked myself what I needed to do next. I picked up my journal and asked myself the same question.

And an extraordinary answer came to me.

'Follow your nose' it said.

At the time I had no idea what this meant, so I hung around in my journal and explored a bit more about my own interests, skills, talents and gifts – the things that were right under my nose.

Immediately I found a reading group that would reconnect me with my interest in literature; I volunteered to write articles for the local parish magazine, to hone my writing skill; I discovered my talent for story-telling by winning first prize in the very first short story competition I entered; I stepped up to air my public-speaking talent at the local philosophical society; and I was head-hunted by a coaching company who wanted to benefit from my gifts in making things happen in a safe and real way.

For too long I'd been doing what I felt was expected of me – trying to run a business the way everyone told me to. By giving myself some space to stop and reflect on what I could truly and authentically contribute when I'm being me, and making full use of my own unique inner resources, I inadvertently created a whole new career and set of opportunities for myself.

So there's something to be said for plate-spinning and juggling. Perhaps it's a new thing to be said, since often we speak about spinning and juggling less, for fear of smashing plates and dropping balls.

Our capacity to live life to the full is only diminished by filling our lives full of stuff that doesn't really energise or inspire us. If we're constantly dancing to the beat of someone else's drum, rather than finding our own truth and our own rhythm, which is to be found right under our nose, then life becomes exhausting and hard work.

Love what you do, and do what you love, and you too will become madly passionate about your life all over again.

Victoria Steel

34. I am an in-house Intellectual Property Counsel.
I dance with Allsorts Adult Ballet group, novice ice-skater.

In-between time

I am somewhere in between young and old at the moment, the no man's land of my mid thirties. I like being here, having learned from my twenties that I will never be truly drop dead gorgeous but also that I can look quite good when I make the effort. I wore aqua marine tights under my black skirt to the office yesterday, which might put me more in one camp than the other depending on your own vantage point.

I am everything, in this middle time, a mother, a daughter, a wife, an ex-girlfriend, a professional woman and a capable party goer. People talk about juggling, wanting to be all things to all people and spreading yourself too thin. I don't recognise these fears. I feel incredibly lucky that I have the opportunity and the means to model and enjoy wearing each of the hats that are on loan to me.

My days vary; I am flexible and extremely fortunate that others around me allow me to be. I start my days early because the more I get done before everyone else gets up, the more time I have with them when they do. I try to ring fence key times and events, whether they are visits to the ice rink or my sons' bath time. If looking at the week ahead my diary is biased too far towards work, I take a day off to re balance. I undertake an ongoing assessment of where and how I commit my time and if I feel unhappy with it or my husband begins to comment, adjustments need to be made.

Would I be a better mum if I didn't work, go to ballet class or ice-skating lessons? – I don't think so. I want to show my boys that life is there for enjoying and that whatever responsibilities or commitments I have, there will always, absolutely be enough of me for them. How successful I am at this is difficult for me to assess but I know how hard I try. I hope that when I am with my family it is for the important times (the play days as we call them as well as the difficult times) and that my sons and I will be well prepared for when they want to and need to live more independently.

The only fear that hides during busy days but sneaks in at night, is that something will be taken away from me, but I imagine that this is a fear that most women share however much or little they have.

—o-O-o—

Amy Rigg

30, Commissioning Editor from Cheltenham, now living with partner and big dog in Gloucester.

All About Books

A typical day for me always starts in the same way: a little whine outside the bedroom door signals me that it's time to wake up and take my Labrador out for her morning walk. I throw on my wellies and an overcoat and we head straight down to the fields. It can be a bit of a struggle in bad weather but I always enjoy it when I'm out there and the views are stunning in the early morning.

A quick breakfast and then I'm driving across the hills to the publishing house where I work, just outside a small Cotswold town. The hills can be treacherous in winter but I always take pleasure in the scenery. Our offices are based in an old Cotswold mill and everyone who visits comments on the building with its warm stone. It's certainly a pleasant place to spend each day.

Once I arrive at work the first port of call is the kettle and then I check the emails that have arrived overnight. There are usually quite a lot of them and getting them out of the way as much as possible is a first priority. Then I'll check my team are getting on OK with their individual projects and plan what else needs doing to ensure our production schedule is on track, before I begin my own work for the day.

I manage a list that publishes around 50 books a year. I'm responsible for commissioning the books and getting the manuscripts in from the authors, and then for overseeing the entire process from the arrival of the manuscript to the finished book coming in from the printers. I liaise with the design department as they come up with covers and internal layouts, and between us my team will edit, proofread and correct each book before sending it to print. I also present each book to our sales reps and marketing department and keep them up to date with relevant materials. It's a busy, fast-paced environment and we have an energetic, vibrant staff around us.

Often I'll have meetings scheduled throughout the day. An author might be bringing in their material or a prospective author coming to discuss their ideas. We have weekly meetings to present new title proposals to our acquisitions panel: we present to the directors and heads of editorial, sales and marketing and there is a lively discussion over the merits of each new book. Often a few new manuscripts arrive to be considered for possible publication and there's always work to be done in evaluating whether the idea is something we can sell effectively.

At the end of each day I have to make a list of things I didn't manage to fit into the day that's just been. There is always a lot to do and plenty to be carried over. While it can be very busy and sometimes quite stressful producing our programme on time and on budget, even the difficult days are interesting. Books are something of a calling to a lot of people and there is often a palpable buzz in the office that comes from a number of people working together on something they enjoy. Most people come to the industry because they are passionate about books and get a real sense of satisfaction from their work. The steady stream of applicants every year certainly proves that a career in publishing still has a wide appeal. While it's not really a glamorous job full of launches and parties – at least, in the countryside it isn't! – it is a lot of fun and I can truly say I love what I do.

Tracy French

38, born in Bristol; I have also lived in Dorset. I spent nine months travelling around the world in 2002 and since then I have been living back in Bristol. I am married to Michael (married 2007), he is German but has been living in Bristol for the last 15 years. We both love Bristol.

Doing Something Worthwhile

My day starts with an alarm at 6.30am, I slowly come to consciousness and check which bits of me feel stiff or painful. I have rheumatoid arthritis (RA); I was diagnosed when I was 30. The diagnosis was terrifying for me, even though I am a nurse, sometimes a little knowledge can be a bad thing! I have, however, been very lucky as I started treatment quickly and although taking rather powerful drugs that suppress my immune system I have been 'in remission' for most of the previous 8 years. Rheumatoid arthritis is when your immune system attacks your body; you get stiff, swollen and painful joints. Even the simplest of tasks such as putting on deodorant can be near impossible, and the mornings are usually the worst.

Michael (my husband) and I have two dogs – Eddy and Elvis, terrier mutts who are brothers and inseparable. We all head off to the park at 8am, me with my bike, and after our walk I cycle the 4km into work. It's a lovely ride initially alongside a river. This is my thinking time for the day. I always say "good morning" to my dad as I ride, he died in 2007, two weeks after my wedding. I am still waiting for it to get easier without him, as everybody tells me it will.

I work at the Bristol Royal Infirmary, my title is Clinical Nurse Specialist, and I work in the Rheumatology Department. So the majority of the people I care for have RA, but none of them know I also have it. I had decided I wanted to specialise in Rheumatology just before I started to get symptoms myself. It was very hard initially, looking at patient's deformed hands and seeing how the RA impacted on their lives and not knowing what my future would hold. RA affects people very differently and I never tell people about my diagnosis, as I can't presume to know exactly what they are going through. They may have more severe disease than mine, or may not have responded so well to the drugs. However, I can empathise with them, which hopefully improves the care I give.

A lot of my working day is spent giving advice and support to patients over the telephone helpline. This sometimes requires a trained instinct to ask the right questions to get the whole picture to identify urgent problems – a lot of it comes down to problem solving. I also run three nurse-led clinics a week. During the consultations with patients I explain their diagnosis (in plain English!), make sure they understand their medication such as possible side effects and what blood tests they need to have done. However, often the consultation will include much more personal conversations about the psychological and social impact of their disease, relationship issues or financial problems. I feel it is a privilege to hold my position and that I am very lucky in that I can build relationships with patients. Positive feedback from patients is wonderful as I feel like I am doing something worthwhile – it is not high drama nursing which used to thrill me when I worked in A&E, but it is just as satisfying. I love my job!

Susan Pready

Lives in Swindon. Started working life as a teacher now a passionate, qualified and experienced Japanese Acupuncture Practitioner since 1986. Also currently Academic Dean Toyohari UK. On European Teaching Team Toyohari.

Happily Healing

Acupuncture is a holistic therapy. The oldest records are around 2,200 years old. It is the primary form of health care for a billion+ people on the planet.

My original interest in it as an effective preventative modality arose from my engineer of a father, who stressed the merit of regular maintenance of all things with moving parts.

I practice acupuncture both from a private practice in Swindon and two clinics in Cardiff. A generalist, I never can imagine the story of the next person needing treatment. Some seek help when all other avenues have failed, others increasingly use it as a way to maintain wellness, fight infection, improve sleep quality, ease stiff and painful joints, stay on top.

I love the variety of my life, the days I wished I stacked shelves are nonexistent. Gladys's fear of water, which keeps her awake, dates from hearing her parents talk about the Titanic (not the film); Jean is desperate to conceive before time runs out; Jenny's tennis elbow prevents her doing her gardening; Jack's neck pain means he has difficulty swinging his golf club; Andy has severe knee pain which stops him working; Richard is still bedwetting age nine; so many migraines, even called to hospital to treat a patient not responding to oral morphine; back pains in all shapes and sizes, sleeplessness, anxiety, depression, tinnitus, Bell's palsy, coughs and colds, asthma, gastric upsets, plantar fasciitis, sciatica. This gentle, sophisticated therapy brings relief and wellbeing

Other days I'm teaching Post Graduate Acupuncture at the University of Westminster, or the Japanese Acupuncture Centre in Amsterdam, sharing my enthusiasm and experience with other committed practitioners. Then there's answering emails, delighted by the text picture of a month old baby whose mother came for treatment, booking appointments, reading through a new case history, talking over difficulties with colleagues

My DREAM is to start a campaign to offer five sessions of acupuncture to all women in the UK on the NHS. If you keep women well, you benefit the family, hence the whole of society. Five because I originally practised Five Element Acupuncture, which comprises five seasons, additionally Late Summer between Summer and Autumn.

Liz Rothschild

Born 1957. Live with partner Adam Twine and two children, Rowan and Laurie. Have worked most of my life engaging different communities through the arts.. Thirty years working in all aspects of theatre, and with performers with learning or physical disabilities; twenty years as a celebrant helping people mark significant stages in their lives; six years with 'Women in Power'. Founder trustee of Root and Branch community project and now also manager of Westmill Woodland Burial Ground.

Too Many Pies

I try to start my day with something physical – a swim, game of tennis, a walk with our dogs, some Tai Chi or other meditative exercise. I find it really helps me especially as I have arthritis which I am working to control with diet. It seems to be working which is wonderful.

So my day will always seem faintly ridiculous because it has always been my weakness to keep my finger in too many pies. All my life I have been involved with the theatre and community arts in different balances at different times. For a long time I was an actor touring around the country, working in reps and then directing and writing. Before that I was part of a team running an arts centre in North Norfolk. When I moved to the Oxfordshire/Wiltshire border to live with my partner Adam Twine and had two children I began to explore developing work locally. This led to seventeen years of directing a theatre company in Swindon for people with learning disabilities and mental health issues called Partners – part of Reach Inclusive Arts – and setting up a range of local projects… So to my day! First off a meeting about the new website for the burial ground at Westmill Farm. I am one of those infuriating people who know exactly what they want things to look like but have no idea what is involved technically in achieving that. Good discipline having to pare down your words, find the right images and think about the effect of this on someone you have never met just randomly coming across your site when looking for information.

Also go up to check our willow bower is rooting and sprouting and keep it watered. We planted it in February – a group of us all with loved ones buried up there. A lovely day of bright sun, kettle on the fire all day and lots achieved including quiet time just to be up there and remember. The sound of larks up there is so lovely and I am really pleased with the bright new sign on the gate. People will be able to find us now! Send some corrections on a eulogy I am working on with a family for a funeral at which I will be the celebrant. A real privilege to be invited into people's lives in this intimate way and develop a funeral that really celebrates the person they have lost.

Meeting about 'Bridging the Gap', my inter-generational project in Faringdon, at the Community College. Excited about getting Year 8s helping elders get the best out of computers and mobile phones. I think this will be a very popular activity and great to extend our work up into the secondary level. So far all our work has been at the junior school. Westmill Sustainable Energy Trust is also developing their website so we are working on providing lots of good materials up there for pupils and teachers so that effective distance learning can take place. The trust is a charity connected to Westmill Windfarm whose brief is to provide education on sustainability locally. Go through our store of photos to choose good ones. Nice job and proud of them because a lot were taken by my daughter, Rowan. We only have small team of volunteers but it is always very rewarding even if it can be a bit blowy up there sometimes. Good thing though really! We are always looking for more recruits by the way.

I go to collect my son, Laurie, off the bus and make sure he has something sensible to eat for supper. I like cooking from scratch and try to eat mainly organic which is easy around here with all the various local producers we have. I also make a big pot of soup to share with a group of women friends who are coming to camp at the weekend. We meet four times a year to mark the seasons and enjoy some relaxing time together in nature. I Skype my daughter who is studying for her International Baccalaureate in Hong Kong at one of the United World Colleges – so many people have not heard of them. We only discovered about them by chance. An amazing opportunity for her.

Bath and bed with a biography because my other preoccupation is finding time to write another one woman show. I know I can't actually start researching and writing until the autumn but I am sowing seeds. My last one was about Rachel Carson. She is a hard act to follow. Such an interesting and dramatic story, she achieved so much and her work on pesticides is still so relevant today. I am on the hunt for my next subject. No doubt there will be some good subjects in this book but they are all alive and well unfortunately! Any suggestions out there?

A woman in
a man's world

A WOMAN IN A MAN'S WORLD

Elaine Arthurs

Born in Chippenham 1978. Always had a passion for history. Degree in History, Postgraduate Diploma in Heritage Studies, now in the museum and heritage profession.

The Railway Archivist

I often wonder how I came to work in a railway museum, full of locomotives, dirty tools and overalls. But my love of social history and fascination with old objects makes me more than qualified to be there! I began working as the Collections Officer at STEAM – Museum of the Great Western Railway in April 2004 after many years of training and volunteering as a museum professional.

My role of Collections Officer means I am responsible for the safety, care and interpretation of the Museum's collection of objects. With such a varied collection of items at STEAM my days at work are never the same.

Today I came into work to a stream of emails. I run the Research and Enquiry service, which at times can be quite intense.My first email enquiry is from a lady researching her family history. Genealogy is a popular subject, and with so many men and women working for the Great Western Railway from the late 1830s until the late 1940s I get many requests come my way. This first enquiry is quite exciting as she is after some information on her great-great Grandfather, William Laverick. After some digging around in our archive and library I was pleased to email back with the news that William was a founder member of the Railway Works in Swindon. He was an important figure and the enquirer was thrilled by the discovery. Unfortunately my own family history research has not uncovered anyone quite as important!

After sifting through a few more enquires I get called to the reception to meet a gentleman who has brought in a donation for the Museum. We get objects donated quite often, and it really helps us build up our knowledge of the railway. Paperwork and photographs are donated regularly, but today's donation has the wow factor! As I greet the donor I can see what looks like a very large object. I'm intrigued to know what it is and soon the object is revealed. It is a very old GWR drop-dial clock and is of huge historical value. The clock came from a station in Somerset and is in excellent condition. I jump at the chance to accept the donation and the gentleman is just pleased that it has gone to a good home. The clock will now get catalogued before going on display in the Museum.

A really great find!

After lunch I head down to some of the Museum stores with the Curator. What we have on display is only a small proportion of what STEAM actually looks after. Both myself and the Curator monitor the environmental conditions of the stores, as well as being on the look out for nasty pests such as clothes moths and carpet beetles! We have recently moved our picture store and need to sort through hundreds of rather large framed photographs, prints and paintings. At the back of the store we find a large framed object which I recognise as the wreath from Queen Victoria's funeral train. It is a rather macabre object, and not strictly a painting or a photograph! But it fits into the store well.

Whilst sorting through the store I get called to the reception again. This time a TV crew have turned up and would like to film inside the Museum. We often get requests like this, as STEAM is the perfect backdrop for railway documentaries. Sometimes, a celebrity presenter will show up which makes it even more exciting, but today it is just the producer and a cameraman. I show them around and point out some of the more interesting parts of the display. There is so much to see that they decide to come back tomorrow.

By the time the TV crew leave, it is also time for me to leave and go home. After such a hectic day I will pop to the gym and then go home and relax. Who knows what tomorrow will bring, but working at STEAM I can guarantee that I will never get bored!

Tina Greening

Age 47, resident of Highworth Wiltshire.

A Lady Butcher

Hi… I'm Tina, I'm forty-seven years of age and I work in a butcher's shop. Yes, a butcher's! For some reason I always get the same reply, "Butcher, an unusual job for a woman"

It isn't really unusual but people still find it strange. I must admit when I was offered the position I actually thought they were having a laugh because I didn't go looking for the job I just walked in and mentioned that I had just been made redundant and I was offered a job there and then. My interview consisted of… "Can you make a decent cuppa? Go and put the kettle on then".

After I made the butchers a cuppa (which, of course was excellent!) I was taken to the office where we had 'a chat'. I had to try on an apron and a straw boater hat (very fetching!) I was asked when could I start and that was the beginning of my new career… Tina the butcher's assistant and that is where my journey begins.

I started at Andrews Quality Meats in March 2000. I was thirty seven years of age with two teenage children. Not married but with a three bedroom house. My first thought was how cold it was, was this actually the right job for me? I soon settled in to my daily routine of firstly making sure everyone had a nice hot cuppa then just generally helping out with the day to day running of a very busy but very friendly butcher's shop. I've never really got involved in the cutting of the meats but I know the basics, which is good enough for me. I was mainly 'front of shop' so soon got to know all the regular customers on a first name basis. "Morning Tina" and I would look up to see a friendly smiling face. "Morning Harry" – or – "Morning Sue".

The amount of people that made the comment of "So nice to have a young lady serving us", as I was the only female working in the shop for a good few years. It was a great boost to my confidence and I got lots of attention, which I thoroughly enjoyed.

After a while we introduced the making and selling of baguettes to the general public which was mainly my responsibility. It took off really well and is still going strong, even though we have a lot of competition in the High Street but it still keeps me very busy.

In 2006 we were asked if we would participate in a 'naked' calendar for Macmillan cancer support. What a laugh that was. There was myself and four butchers with only our aprons to protect our modesty with our bare bottoms proudly on display. The picture was taken on a cold October morning whilst the shop was open. All for a good cause though.

Apparently our 'bottoms' adorn many a kitchen wall to this very day!

I have seen a lot of staff come and go in my ten years at Andrews, sadly, a lot of customers also as some are quite elderly and you get to know them so well. It's very upsetting when you hear that one of them has passed away.

In June 2005 my partner decided to leave me. I won't go into detail but my bosses Andy and Andy were my rock. I had endless amounts of time off work when I felt I couldn't face anyone; I felt I just couldn't cope with what had become the 'daily routine' of my life.

I soon realised that they weren't just my employers but my friends and they both helped me work through the really difficult stages of my break up. I actually found it easier talking to them than I did to my own family. They were the ones that helped me get my life back on track and here I am today. Still here at Andrews Quality Meats.

I actually love my job. Always meeting new people, friends. I wouldn't change it for the world.

Janet Hyde

49. Single. Have been living in the Greater London area all my life apart from three university years in Bristol (which feels like my second home).

"See Ya Toots!"

Growing up as a teenager in the 1970s, when feminism took flight, I always assumed that I had as much right to an education and a career as anyone else, to be treated as an equal and accorded the respect that I was taught to give others. It was not until I decided to go into banking and found myself in the City in the early 1980s that this assumption began to be challenged. Within days of starting my first job I was 'fondled' by an inconsequence of a man but discovered I was wholly ill-equipped to deal with the affront. Gradually, I realized that equality in the workplace was not to be taken for granted. Lunching in the furthest reaches of the City several years later, where the shipping companies and insurance firms still tend to congregate, I happened to look beyond our table around the packed restaurant and noticed, slack-jawed, that I was the only woman there.

My clients are trading companies, moving oil and gas, metals and agricultural commodities around the world. To me, trade makes the world go round and my work has proved endlessly fascinating over the years. However, it can be a hard-drinking, foul-mouthed, testosterone-fuelled environment in which to work. The edges have been softened over the decades by legislation and political correctness and I have had the great pleasure to work with some intelligent and professional gentlemen. But the core remains, largely hidden from view, and even in the 21st century women remain very much in the minority. The steel trading fraternity is perhaps most rooted in the past. Not so long ago, I remember entering one client's office where staff with names like Wally (not as a pejorative term then) leafed through bundles of documents in a fug of cigarette smoke. I was called 'dear' by only one of their number although, more amusingly, a New York client once signed off our phone call with "See ya, toots". I doubt my male colleagues have been addressed as a gangster's moll but I guess they (and I) have been called worse behind our backs.

Which brings me to my point. Not all women are great to work with either. A female CEO recently dispensed of my services by e-mail rather than explaining her quite reasonable situation to me face to face the day before. And it was also only in the last decade that I had to deal with a posse of four female secretaries who did their best to undermine me on a daily basis in small, mealy-mouthed ways – I see working women treat each other in this way often – feeling I suppose that my male colleagues offered them more status. In fact, one of these paragons made a formal complaint about me – because my bonus was higher than his. This was supposed to be a confidential matter but, then again, my (male) boss was his best mate at the time. It wasn't until 2001 when two female Asian colleagues said I had 'presence' that I felt I was finally finding my poise.

I've lost count of the number of men I've met who carve their careers solely on the basis of humour and charm or complete obfuscation and procrastination, and yet struggle to think of any women who deploy the same traits in order to succeed. If anything, the most ambitious and determined appear to adopt the steeliness and self-absorption of the slick-suited majority. But I believe women have more to lose in this approach: their convictions, values and sensibilities add the human dimension to a results-orientated business world. A working environment dominated by either men OR women would be a miserable and far less productive place to be.

I recently had a conversation with the highly intelligent and accomplished husband of a very dear friend, both of us thwarted by a vicious recession despite our considerable international commercial experience. I described how I missed meeting interesting people who know what is going on in the world, the stimulating interaction with my colleagues from all parts of the globe, the dignity and purpose that work provides, the ability to take care of myself. "Nah", he said, "I just want to be a B-- S------- D---."

Jen Steiner

Born 1981, from various places in England. Lived in Bristol for over a year. In a long-term lesbian relationship. I am a feminist, a musician, an artist, and a gardener.

A Woman in a Man's World – That's Every Woman, Isn't It?

1   Our world is a man's world, based mostly on greed, exploitation, profit, fear and hopelessness.Could this ever be the work of women? I don't think so.

2   Today is Saturday. I'm a young woman living in Britain, and today I'm thinking about hopelessness.

3   It is not the hopelessness of watching my people being killed, threatened or taken by force. It is not the hopelessness of waiting for rains that will never come. It is not the hopelessness of not being able to feed my family. It is not the hopelessness of my body being violated or abused. It is a subtle hopelessness.

4   In the place and in the time I live this hopelessness seems to be everywhere, even my beliefs appear to have been invaded. This subtle hopelessness tries to convince me that it makes no difference to myself or the world if I speak out against injustice or domination, to a man or a woman, that it will make no difference at all.

As a woman I am expected, without fail, to ignore and accept quietly, all aspects of sexism and male domination. I am supposed to be silent, sexy, and to smile at men's lewd remarks or gestures. I am supposed to use my body to please men. I am supposed to believe sexism doesn't even exist.

5   I feel sad today. A friend of mine told me his brother had been found dead in his flat. I listened to him crying on the telephone. I cried too.

6   Later I went to a local park with another male friend and we decided to climb a tree.

7   I stood underneath the tree and jumped up, grabbing the lowest branch with both my hands. I began to lift my body off the floor and up onto the branch, but my arms didn't feel strong enough, it felt hopeless. I let go and landed on the ground. I looked up at tree. I didn't want to give up.

8   My friend was wiggling his way up the tree confidently.

9   I jumped again, catching the branch in both my hands, and using the jump from my legs and the strength of my arms I lifted my body up, then I swung my feet and legs up over the branch and pulled the rest of me up so I was sitting upright on the branch.

I felt a little scared, as I often do when I use my body past the point I think I can. I stood up, supporting myself in the embrace of the tree and its branches, and began to climb higher up.

10 My friend and I lay back on high branches, trusting the tree to hold our weight and began to talk. I told my friend how scary it can feel to use the power of my body. He told me he'd spent all of his school life in same sex education, all male, he told me some things he is scared of too.

11 I watched him swinging from a branch, his legs dangling. I enjoyed the feeling of the tree, swinging its body with ours. I reached out my hand and so did he, the tips of our fingers met and I felt glad of the connection we have.

12 It means a lot to me as a young woman to have as friends young men who are not always afraid to cry or to show their feelings. It makes a difference.

13 I began to feel not quite so hopeless, not quite so lonely. Then I came home and wrote this to you.

Judy Hall

Lives in Minehead.

Working on the Railway

My name is Judy Hall and I work in the Buffer Stop Shop at Minehead Station on the West Somerset Railway. Previously I worked in the Booking Office, and have been working at the railway for twelve years.

My typical day begins with preparing the shop for the day ahead. We open up and put out all the postcard stands and signs. Then we start to meet (and chat to) the first customers of the day, many of whom will be travelling on the railway.

The phone messages are checked and dealt with as is the post. We quite often receive phone orders from customers and we also have an online shop, these purchases are carefully wrapped and made ready to send.

Sometimes, we will get an order from another station shop along the line, this has to be picked and boxed up, then sent down on the next train to the relevant station.

We have deliveries of stock arriving most days, these have to be checked, unpacked, priced up and then put on the shelves for sale.

The first train of the day arrives mid-morning and this is quite often a busy time so we get ready to welcome the passengers and assist them with any enquiries.

We meet a large variety of different people – day-trippers, coach parties, families, holiday makers and steam enthusiasts wanting to travel behind one of our engines.

There is also a team of volunteers who come in and work in the shop, which is especially useful when it's busy.

After taking a break for a quick lunch, which are taken in turn, we tidy the shop and re-stock the shelves ready for the afternoon passengers. A lot of passengers like to buy a souvenir of their visit before going home.

Towards the end of the day, if there is a quiet moment, I'll vacuum and tidy the shop, and then it's time to get ready to close, bringing in the stands and signs, serving the final customers of the day and lastly cashing up.

Laura Jane Bulgarelli

Aged 18, live in Wroughton near Swindon. Single.

It's Different, and I Like It!

If I'm honest, the afternoon my mother came home and told me she'd got me an interview for work in a hardware shop, I wasn't too impressed. It was the first formal interview I'd ever been offered in my life, and if I succeeded my first proper job too.

I'd never pictured myself in a working environment before, especially one that I was unable to relate to. I remember my dad dropping me off to do my first shift in late November. It was a cold, miserable, wet afternoon, and there was me stood outside this little hardware store, which at the time looked massive and totally unfamiliar.

Taking my first few steps, and standing there inside the doorway, I was noticed by my boss Dan who formally introduced to me to Steve his colleague and friend. At the time the store was dealing with a large stock intake and the first job given to me was pricing door mats. As I knelt down with a plastic red pricing gun, and what seemed like more than enough mats to price! I began to look around the place I would be working within over the coming months. It all seemed so detailed, so many products in different places, which all did different things for different jobs for different reasons, and I was going to have to learn it all! At the time it seemed unachievable for someone like me, but I did achieve it while finding out what it means to work for something.

Having my first job changed a lot for me, I do find it funny how one change can affect you so much, even if it's small. I know now that you only get out what you put in and sometimes, you do have to work hard for it. I find I've come to admire those types of people and am hopeful and sure that the best things will happen to them.

I realise my job may not be the most fabulous or glamorous one a woman could ask for, but I will say this, it's different and I like that. I've met some pretty nice people who are all individual and brilliant in their own way, so I would like to thank all of them for teaching me I am a woman who can survive in a man's world.

A special day

A SPECIAL DAY

Kate Montgomery

Professional name Katherine Newman: born in the Steel Works town of Corby but grew up in the Wiltshire countryside. Ten years at an all girls convent school. Trained at Queen Margaret Drama School, Edinburgh. Professional actress for eight years. Now living and working in London and around the world.

Making Magic

It was Sunday, 6.30 am and the alarm was going off. My body was in shock. Having been working in a bar for months, this side of the day was for saying 'goodnight' rather than 'good morning'. I promptly hit the snooze button.

I had come to London two years previously to pursue my career as an actress. It had been going 'so-so': a theatre tour, some play readings, a few nice parts in some films. Other times there were jobs to stay afloat: Champagne waitress, call centre worker, teaching assistant, flyerer, fashion guru (don't ask!). Today was a new job – tenuously related to my chosen career – I was to be a Magical Fairy.

After a long shower I packed my tool-box:

Fairy costume and wand – check. Hats for Goblin, Prince, Witch, Wizard and Queen – check. Tin whistle, music, magic cloth, sweets, stickers, sparkle dust – check. Lack of pride – check. Large bottle of Pinot Grigio cooling in the fridge for return – CHECK! I was good to go.

I was met at the village hall by the slightly crazed Mother who, on realizing I was the entertainment, flung her arms around me saying, "Oh, thank God you're here. I would have died if I had to entertain the little rascals all by myself". She offered me a glass of Champers with the comment, "Well my daughter's only going to be four once." Although very tempted, I declined the alcohol in favour of being a sober, albeit slightly terrified, fairy.

I crammed myself into the broom-cupboard-cum-dressing-room, to don gold sparkly dress and more glitter than is appropriate for a drag act. I emerged to pandemonium – kids everywhere, sliding across the floor, screaming, and generally causing mayhem. I took a deep breath, flew over to my CD player and pressed Play. The fairy music started and I began to sing. I say sing, it was more a mortifying muddle of nervous squeaks.

Slowly each child came and sat down in front of me. "Who are you?" they asked. "What's your name? Are you a real fairy?" These little cuties instantly believed that this nervous twenty-six year old lady was, in fact, Sugar-Toes the Dancing Fairy. They believed she had specifically come to Iona's birthday to recruit other fairies to venture into the Magical Forest to find the Mean Old Witch and make her take back all the nasty spells she had inflicted over the Fairy Kingdom. These were the children who were on my side. Max, Harry and Angus, however, were not.

Max "You're not a real fairy!"

Harry "Yeah! Fairies don't exist!"

Angus "You're just a teenager dressed up in a fairy costume!"

Now, as delighted as I was to be mistaken for a teenager, I was well aware of the problems these non-believers could cause.

"OK," I said. "You don't have to believe in me, but we are all going on a wonderful adventure and we need brave young men like you to help and protect us."

"Whatever", they exclaimed in chorus, and got back to their game of whacking each other in the face with balloons.

So I began my story with the rest of the children in tow. There were gasps at the powers of the invisible cape, a flurry of "Me, me," to be a character in the forest, a few tears of fear at the mention of the Witch and some wonderful displays of flying around the room that would make any fully–grown up fairy proud.

Finally each child sat in a circle with their eyes closed and hands held out to receive some magic dust so they could make a wish. To my surprise, there were the three non-believers. As I placed the dust in their palms I gave a little smile.

The party was over! I was exhausted. I felt a little tug on my wings.

"You really are a real fairy," said Harry as he flung his arms around me smiling. "When I grow up, I want to be a magical fairy and live in the Adventure Forest just like you!"

Although not quite a play at the RSC or the lead as Johnny Depp's love interest, this job did teach me a thing or two – about the beauty of the imagination, the wonderful and honest inquisitive nature of children and the importance of letting yourself believe. That day also taught me that there is a little magic in us all.

Linda Treadwell

48, born Speyside, now residing in beautiful county of Moray. Working mother of two. Loves to be fit — walks, cycles, visits gym, also canoes, and climbs (sometimes). Passion — gardening. Ambition — to visit as many European and world renowned gardens as possible!

A Dream Day in Morocco

On our first morning on holiday in Marrakech, I awoke very early with the haunting sound of the Muslim call to prayer drifting faintly from the Koutoubia Mosque towards our hotel. I was excited about what awaited us to experience in a different country and culture.

We had many plans to explore this city and our first stop was close to our hotel, the Jardin Majorelle, to satisfy my passion for gardens. As it was November, the warmth of the sun was most welcome. The contrast between the dry dusty city streets to the lush oasis of exotic green plants and trees was magical and we both appreciated this haven of beauty and tranquillity. The plants within the garden were much bigger and more colourful than I had expected. The blue colour of the buildings were the most intense shade and contrasted beautifully with their surroundings. These few hours were the start of a wonderful day.

It was still early, so we took a coach trip to Essaouria on the Atlantic coast. On the way, we stopped at one of many Women's Co-operatives throughout Morocco which produces Argan Oil from the nut trees. My husband Ray was invited to take part in grinding the nuts to extract the oil. We had a tour of the premises by one of the ladies. We purchased some oil and honey and thanked the workforce before we had to get back on the coach.

On arrival in Essaouira, it looked completely different being on the Atlantic coast. We made our way to the harbour area then explored the ramparts which are of Portuguese origin. It has a fascinating history and still relies on it's fishing and tourist industries. Having spotted some camels and their keepers on the beach, we walked over to negotiate a fifteen minute camel ride across the dunes. This was such great fun. Not quite a trek across the Sahara, but really enjoyable. The men were very willing to take photos for us. They were very accommodating and had a lovely sense of humour. Before we left, we shared a laugh and joke with them. It was agreed that Ray had to 'barter' with the men. I was to be exchanged for one of the camels. Ray joked that it was a fair exchange!

By now, we were hungry and sought some food back in the town. We headed back towards the harbour area and began to smell the aroma of food. As if planned, we had arrived in time to enjoy daily barbecues. The fishermen sell their catch to the public. We chose the fish and waited to be served. A large platter of freshly barbecued fish arrived served with salad and crusty bread washed down with a chilled lemonade. After briefly exploring the souks and alleyways, we had to rendezvous with the coach to take us back to Marrakech.

On arrival back in the city late afternoon, we took a Caleche ride out to the Menara Gardens to watch the sunset over the Atlas Mountains. We walked thru' the Olive groves to the Pavilion where we had an elevated view of the panorama. There certainly are many sights to experience and enjoy in Morocco. We walked back up the Avenue of flowers and fountains to the famous Jemaa el Fna Square which is transformed from a traders market place during the day to a night market selling lots of delicious food. The musicians, street performers and snake charmers appeared and all added to the vibrant atmosphere of the city. The whole square was truly alive. We 'soaked' up the a marvellous sights of the medieval pageant around us while eating a Lamb Tagine.

By now it was getting late and we finally headed back to our hotel in the French sector. We stopped on the way at a modern area of the city which is more European in style, to enjoy a coffee and pastry. We began to unwind and discuss all the delights of our first full day in and around Marrakech. We had so many more unique events to savour and enjoy in Morocco.

Beth Lodwick
Race Day

If someone had told me last year that I'd be sitting here grinning ear to ear having completed the Great South Run, a 10 mile race through Portsmouth, I would have thought they were crazy. This time one year ago I could barely get through the day without collapsing in floods of tears. I picked up a tropical disease on my honeymoon which left me suffering from chronic daily headaches for eighteen months after the holiday. I still have minor headaches now, and when I told my family about my mad cap plan to take part in the race they expressed their concerns as I am still recovering. This didn't stop me.

It was a couple of months ago that one of my Twitter friends invited me to take part in the run. To be honest my conscience made me sign up because it was in aid of MS Research (Multiple Sclerosis Research Training and Education), a charity close to my heart. My logical side kicked in "surely I can run 10 miles, it can't be that hard can it?".

After a short period of training, race day soon came around. I was really nervous at the starting line, the other runners all looked so much more experienced than me. It started getting tough at the half way mark but I focussed on my headache hell last year and that spurred me on. My sister always says I have immense strength of mind and it was definitely my mind which ran the race for me.

My final time was 1 hour 26, I was over the moon with this. I didn't think a time like that was achievable for me. I will never forget the immense sense of pride I felt crossing the finishing line.

For me, my race day was a turning point in my headache recovery. If my headaches are bad now, I think of my achievements on that day and it makes me smile.

Sally Willson

Mother of five, grandmother of three happy step-grandmother of one, nurse, active member of the Community Church, Highworth.

Remembering Jean

My name is Sally and I've been married to Mike for thirty years. We have been blessed with two sons and three daughters none of whom currently live at home but are still a large part of my busy life. I work part- time as a nurse in a community clinic in Swindon. I am also a member of a Christian community church in the historic Wiltshire market town where we've lived for twenty five years.

Last Friday I was due to drive down to Portsmouth in the afternoon to pick up my five year old granddaughter and my nearly three year old grandson from school and nursery (my middle daughter's two children). Two days before this I heard of the unexpected death of Jean. The memorial service was in Shirley Baptist Church Southampton on Friday morning so I was able to arrange to attend en route. I am so glad I did this because it was such a wonderful tribute to a faith filled vivacious life which although very emotional (I'm going through that hormonal phase of life which women of my age will identify with), was also profoundly challenging.

Jean had been part of that church for seventy-two of her eighty -one years, had met her husband there and brought up her two daughters there. She was still putting her organisational skills to great use and will be sorely missed by that community. I met Jean's younger daughter Jenny in 1976 when we started our nurse training at Guys hospital. We became good friends and along with two other girls lived and holidayed together. We all four went on to train as midwives.

I'd been married for a year and just had my eldest son when Jenny went out to New Zealand to work as a midwife. Tragically she was killed in a car crash a few months later, just before her 25th birthday. It was one of those unfathomable losses which deeply shocked so many people. There was a service in New Zealand but her body was flown home and I attended her service at the same church in Southampton twenty eight years ago. Much of the tribute to Jean was to how her unshakable faith helped her to weather that storm and carry on with a deep love for God and interest in others.

I was always pleased to hear from Jean as she wrote such upbeat letters and was always interested in my growing family. When another of my Guy's friends tragically lost her own beautiful nineteen year old daughter two years ago in a similar car crash, Jean wrote to her fully empathizing in her pain, sorrow and bewilderment.

After the service I found my way to my youngest son's digs as he is studying music at Southampton University. He was busy composing a piece of music for an assignment. It was lovely to see him and meet four out of his five housemates. They were a very welcoming bunch of lively young people. I was then able to drive on to Portsmouth, pick up my precious grandchildren and enjoy my babysitting duty!

None of us know what days are mapped out before us. My own dear father is gripped in the cruel clutches of dementia and immobilised by Parkinsons. My faithful mother is struggling on as his full time carer. The words of a verse which was read at Jenny's service in New Zealand and which were printed on Jean's service sheet sum up my rambling thoughts:

The Perfect Tapestry

The pattern of our lives is formed
With tender loving care
And He who does the weaving
Works in colours dark and fair
We see odd strands of colour
As the tapestry unfolds
Not understanding why there must be
Greys among the gold
But in the Master Weaver's eye
The whole design is clear
For he alone knows where and when
The dark threads must appear
And if we trust his guiding hand
Then one day we shall see
The final picture woven
In the Perfect Tapestry.

Samantha Lyth

44, have lived in York for most of that time, except for three years at College in Merseyside and ten years in the Scottish Borders. I am married with two teenage children.

The Show Must Go On

I lost my mother a long time ago. My real Mum that is: the one who was my best friend; the one that made me laugh and bolstered my ego and acted as a taxi service; the one who was a shoulder to cry on and the one who believed in me. She faded away gradually and was lost in the dementia-like life that arose from an inoperable brain tumour.

She died earlier this year. Her last gift to us was three lovely weeks with the family at her bedside at home. It was a time of laughter and memories as we spent a lot of time together.

The day in my life I am going to re-count is the day of her funeral. Mum died at 65 with the tumour shadowing the last fifteen to twenty years. But we were determined her funeral would be a celebration of a 'Life well lived'.

Mum's two wishes were to have a Quaker-like ceremony and that we should all dress brightly. Dad put together a programme for the service. He never does anything by halves and the programme he assembled was lovely. Mum's brother was to lead the service with various other people contributing. Music was a huge part of Mum's life and we spent ages selecting relevant music.

A beautiful May morning dawned and everyone donned their brightest clothes, looking more like a wedding party than a funeral party. My sister and I both picked large bunches of flowers from our gardens as Mum always loved the natural look.

After a luxurious trip in a limo behind the hearse we arrived to a packed and brightly coloured crematorium. Standing room only. We entered the room to the music of Arthur

Sullivan. It all ran smoothly. Each piece of music was introduced and relevance explained. Dad read a list of thanks. My sister read about 'A life well lived' celebrating a life of achievement – from riding in the oldest horse race in England to driving a steam train, many of which Mum did after her cancer diagnosis.

I spoke about a 'Life well loved" finishing off with Jenny Joseph's poem 'Warning' - "When I am an old woman I shall wear purple'. All the readings were pertinent and the humour added made it all the more poignant. The funeral director said that he had never heard so much laughter at a funeral!

In the latter weeks of Mum's illness her recent memory had gone, but she could remember poems from her youth, so my daughter read Edward Lear's 'The Jumblies' one of the poems Mum most enjoyed.

We had some time for people to give their own tributes to Mum. It was moving that so many people did this. It is not easy to stand up in front of a packed hall and speak. Mum's friend from school who read 'The Prayer of St Francis.' must have had the most difficult reading, especially the line 'it is in dying that we are born to Eternal Life'.

There was only one choice for the final song: Queen's 'The Show Must Go On". We did not want the curtains closing on the coffin, we wanted Mum to be at the party to the very end – she always liked to be the last to leave!

Outside the crematorium there was a massive re-union: family, singers, nurses, cricketers. They were all there. Many went back to a splendid party in my Aunt's garden. What a pleasure to catch up with so many people, to talk about the person Mum had been before her illness. She would have loved this party

Ingeborg Knight

Born 1939 followed by a life that has been a series of life-changing escapades not least escaping to the West during World War Two and escaping from violent first husband. Have now lived in England for some thirty years. Have one son and daughter and three grandsons.

Finding Mother

Each day is connected to this particular day – both before and since and this is the day I would like to share with you. That day – a sunny day in Prague in October 2005 – brought closure to the life shattering events, some sixty years earlier, at the end of the war and had a profound effect on our lives. It was on that autumnal day when we (my twin sister and I, our brother, half brother and half sister) had at last found and were standing by our mother's grave. It was emotional beyond belief.

To both me and my twin sister, the horrific events of 1945 that led to our being forced to abandon our mother were flashing back in our minds, but here, we had at last found the place where our dear mother was buried giving us both relief and inner peace at having found it. There in front of us was the place where mother was buried albeit with three other females, one only two years old, one just eighteen and a woman of eighty-five. Our mother was just thirty-one years old when she died in June 1945.

It was in June 1945 that we had had to leave her on the edge of the forest, saying goodbye for the last time, hoping of course that she would be taken care of and be able to join us later, safe and well at our home in Lower Silesia – formerly part of Germany but now Poland.

It was almost surreal to find her last resting place and whilst our hearts were heavy, we were so relieved to know that she had not been alone all of those sixty years but accompanied by three others who had also lost their lives at the end of that terrible war – or rather as a result of it.

So we stood there, in that beautiful forest, surrounded by Silver Birches and Pines – a simple cross marking the grave. It was Professor Rychetsky, a historian, whose research had led to the discovery of this near secret place where our journey had led us on that day in 2005 – so far from where we lived. This is the Czech Republic (formerly Czechoslovakia) we were visiting – myself, my sister and her family. Our heartfelt thanks go out to the people who had made that day possible. We had endured many long years of not knowing what had happened to our mother after we had left her there, on the edge of the forest, ill, unable to move, just hoping for kind people to take her to hospital. It left a permanent vacuum in our lives. She had had to send us, her five children, on a desperate journey, some several hundred kilometres to the east through war-torn countries to our home and birthplace in Lower Silesia. My sister and I were just six years old and without shoes, food or water. That journey and the terrible events before were flashing through our minds as we stood in another part of that impenetrable Bohemian Forest.

We took the opportunity of visiting the surroundings of Humpolec, about 100 km west of Prague and the hometown of Professor Rychetsy who had made possible what the Red Cross had failed to achieve in those sixty years. He recounted many an event of those days when thousands of people were fleeing the brutality of the immediate weeks after 9 May 1945.

That day, the day in my life, allows me to think of my dear mother resting in a peaceful place surrounded by beautiful trees – something that many of the casualties of the war were unable to do.

So, for me, this is the one day in my life that I would want to share with you.

Anne Moody

Born West Hartlepool 1921. Passed scholarship but left early as needed to bring money in. Worked as packer in Cerebos Salt Factory. Conscripted in war as welder. Widowed but married over forty years to Harry. Four children (one deceased) six grandchildren and three great grandchildren. Still dote on my family and welcome tiny new members with love and enthusiasm

Mam's Mistake!

A new baby is a glorious event and recently we welcomed Harry James Frederick Lindsey into our family. A bonny, bouncing boy at over 9lb, he was delivered safely in hospital as most babies are these days. So different to my day when the norm was a home delivery. He was born in September of 2010 and with his birth I remembered my own September baby.

I am going back to mid September, the year 1953, one of the many days that stand out in my life. This was one that finished up a joyous day.

I woke up to beautiful sunshine, being a Sunday all was quiet and peaceful. Our two sons, Colin seven years and Fred three and a half, were still asleep. My husband Harry and my mother, who was staying with us awaiting the birth of my third child, were also in the land of nod.

I decided to get up and enjoy the lovely sunshine, peace and tranquillity before the family arose. I decided to have a cup of tea and lo and behold my contractions started to kick in. The two boys came down, I told Colin to get washed and dressed while I attended to Fred, then they went into the garden to play. I took Harry and my Mother a cup of tea and told them what a lovely morning they were missing. I didn't mention I was in the early stages of labour.

I returned downstairs and had my cup of tea. I started setting the table and cooking the breakfast which on a Sunday was the full English. By the time it was ready Mother and Hubby arrived downstairs, the boys came in and we all enjoyed a hearty meal.

By mid morning my Mother and Father-in-law arrived and we all had had a cup of tea or coffee and biscuits. We had a nice chat and I then informed them I was in labour. By late afternoon I decided it was time to send for the midwife. She duly arrived and examined me and told me I would go a few more hours yet. She then told me she would not be attending the birth herself later on, she would be sending a newly qualified midwife in her place. I was to be her first delivery. I must not send for her until the contractions were stronger and more frequent. I had never met her or even knew her name, unheard of today when everyone is on first name terms!

The time arrived for her to be sent for. There were no mobiles, then and we didn't even have a phone, so Harry had to go to a public phone box. Time passed, getting on for forty-five minutes and no midwife came. I called for my Mother and told her my baby was not going to wait. She ended up delivering the baby and fortunately so as the baby had the umbilical cord around its neck which she quickly sorted out. Mam said we had another son and Harry woke the boys up and told them they had a new baby brother.

Eventually the midwife arrived and attended to me and the baby. She said "you have a baby daughter not a baby son". I can understand the mistake my Mother made as she was very worried and concerned.

Exactly three years previously she had lost a beloved daughter and grandchild in childbirth; I say God bless her for her courage.

"Thank you Mam for a beautiful daughter".

Barbara Rawlings

Born in 1928, worked many places abroad, now lives in Warwickshire.

Tandem Hang Gliding

The only thing of any consequence in my 21st Century is when I reached 80 years old. Having a sense of adventure I had already flown in a helicopter, in a small airplane over the United Arab Emirates, had a flight in a Sesna airplane over the Wild Coast of Africa, also a flight over the Grand Canyon National Park, and experienced gliding and hot air ballooning, so I wanted to do something different. I decided to do 'Tandem Hang Gliding' and, instead of presents, get sponsorship for The Warwickshire and Northampton Air Ambulance for which I raised £1,500.

The adventure was actually on my birthday which was a lovely sunny Saturday (we had very few in 2008). I was excited and not at all nervous. I was asked if I wanted to take out insurance, but was not going to waste money, however the extra amusement was that I was sponsored for £299.00 by a local Funeral Director who had just opened near my house and wanted to get involved with the local community. Needless to say he did not get any finance from the deal, but whenever I had the chance I mentioned his kind action.

I was fitted into a garment that went over my body and feet with a hook for hanging me on the hang glider). It was difficult for the pilot to hang me and hook on so my son helped, (good job I had lost weight!). There was a bar in front that I could hang on to as I was in a perpendicular position. This was quite tiring as I had to wait for the pilot to get ready. I then went on top of him put one arm round his shoulder and the other on his clothes just under his belt. Before we started a check had to be made by someone else calling out had he checked various aspects. The video, taken by the company, was started and then I was towed up by a microlite one mile high before being released

The towing part was quite noisy with the microlite and wind. My first impression was that it had turned misty, then I realised we were high above the clouds and it was rather cold. Once we were released it became warmer and my hands started to thaw out. The view of course was magnificent. One forgets how much of England is unspoilt. Whilst we were slowly descending we turned to the right and then the left, which was exhilarating. The landing was the other side of the airport because of the thermals and was very good and gentle like in a real aeroplane.

When I got back the group of thirty five close relations and friends were pleased to see my safely landed (I had had no qualms) and we celebrated with champagne and birthday cake.

It was a wonderful day and the best birthday I had ever had. Everyone asks I what am doing each year. For my 85th perhaps a 'giro copter' or a Harley Davies motor bike ride (as I do like riding motor bikes) and for my 90th I will go up in a micro-lite. It all depends on my state of health, which at the moment is very good. I feel sure my spirit of adventure will be the same.

'Old Age' is an attitude of the mind. I have never thought of me being old. If I have been unable to do anything I never blame my age – try another day. Be positive, eat good food and exercise the mind and body and all will be well.

Wendy Smith

Age 54, born in Surrey, brought up in Bognor Regis, live in Highworth. Married with two grown up children, have two grandchildren. Runner and cyclist by choice..

Running thoughts

Nobody would describe me as athletic – not by any stretch of the imagination. I am short, not thin and hated sports at school – PE seemed to involve hitting/throwing/catching things, which I have never been good at, or doing things fast – also not my thing. Pupils seemed to be separated into those who were brilliant at everything, and were encouraged by teachers, and those who were not and were ignored. I was one of the latter.

So, what am I doing here?. It was Adrian's fault. It started with short runs to the gym. I enjoyed the gym, even after I heard someone say "you should see the girl up in the gym, she's only this big and has thighs like this!", and the run was a warm up to get there. Gradually the runs have got longer.

You think of all sorts of things when running. When not concentrating on any pains you might have – shin splints, Achilles problems, jogger's nipple – you can sort out everyone's life. When running with others, it's amazing the subjects which are covered. Someone once said they thought the reason people talked about all sorts of things on runs, was because you didn't have to look the other person in the eye. Interesting!

Anyway, back to today. After all the preparations, we stayed overnight to get here early. Up in time for breakfast and plenty of trips to the loo – you can never go to the loo too many times before a race. In fact do I need to go again now? No, the queue is too long!

We're off – at least, those at the front are. I am quite a long way back so nowhere near the start.

Eight minutes later… Just reached the start! I must remember to take eight minutes off my finish time to account for that. We are now officially racing although there are so many people, we are still walking. Would be quite a nice pace to do the race at but I might not finish today if I did.

At fifteen miles now… a bit depressing as we have only done just over half way. Also the course goes round the Isle of Dogs here and there aren't many spectators. Time I used the Portaloo but there is a queue. Adrian will never believe it when I tell him I spent two minutes queueing for the loo. He'll say I should have gone behind a bush, but there aren't too many of those out here.

At nineteen miles and the end is not far. There is a young bloke ahead whose legs are about as long as I am tall, and I seem to be gaining on him… Overtaking him now, which makes up for being overtaken by ostriches and the like.

As I am around the five hour mark according to the race clock (mustn't forget to take that eight minutes off), they are beginning to pack up the carpet over the cobbles. It strikes me that that is when they should be putting the carpet down. The fast ones at the front don't need the carpet, but those who are taking several hours could do with a bit of comfort!

Coming up to five miles to go – that's only a quick trip round Fresden and I do that a lot. Mind you I haven't usually done twenty-one miles already! Keep hearing people shout "Well done Wendy" "Go on Wendy". Surely I can't know that many people here. Not far to go now and gaining on those Army chaps who run round with huge packs on their backs. Just turned round and realised the woman behind me has Wendy written on her t-shirt!

Coming up to the finish line and finally reached the end. Time to get the medal and the chocolate bar. Adrian and the boys will be around here to greet me and I hope, to congratulate me.

I may not have broken any records, I may have been beaten by thousands of people, but I have just achieved something I never would have dreamt of achieving all those years ago in PE lessons: I have just completed the 26 miles 385 yards – that is The London Marathon.

Carol Williams

Live with partner and youngest son; one married son and one daughter. Juggle several part-time jobs including working on hospital switch-board.

My Son's Wedding

I woke very early, extremely excited and nervous. Thankfully the sun was shining as I got out of bed. My hair was being cut and styled at 9 am, so, after a shower I made my way to the hairdresser's. While I was there I thought about my son Dean and how happy I was feeling for him that day. Thankfully the hairdresser listened to my request that I didn't want too much cut off my hair – they don't always do they? – and I left there feeling very pleased with the result.

Back at home it was hectic as both my sons were getting themselves ready. I hoped my dress and jacket still looked nice. I got dressed and ready. Luckily it was fine and both my sons and my partner said I looked nice.

My youngest son Michael, who was being 'Best Man,' then left home to go and collect his girlfriend, whilst I and my partner Andy, and Dean then left home to go to Cirencester Registry Office.

I then began to worry about things. Had I forgotten anything? Did Michael have the rings? I spent the next twenty minutes of the journey going through everything in my head over and over again to make sure we hadn't forgotten anything. Dean sat in the back of the car looking incredibly nervous. When we arrived at the Registry Office car park we met some of Dean's friends. This was good because they chatted and laughed with us and I'm sure it helped Dean feel more at ease. I took some photos of the boys together; it seemed amazing how they had all grown up into young men having known them since they were eight years old!

Then we were ushered into the Registry Office and at last Michael and his girlfriend arrived. Thankfully he did have the rings. Dean and Michael sat at the front while we all filed into the seats behind them. I looked around and thought what a lovely place it was. I felt really proud of my sons as they both stood there waiting for Kim and her father to enter the room. Kim looked amazing. She wore a long ivory dress with a small tiara in her hair. I then looked behind Kim and her father and saw my daughter Joanne who was a bridesmaid. She had a long dark dress on and her long dark hair was brushed to one side with flowers in it. She looked lovely. I felt so proud of my daughter, especially when she looked over at me and smiled and she walked down the aisle.

I then listened to the service and saw the look of love in Dean's and Kim's eyes as they said their vows. It was very moving. I was then asked to go to the front of the room and be a witness with Kim's mum.

After the service I was so relieved it had all gone well and Dean and Kim were now married. Outside the Registry Office it was time for the photographs and now I was thinking "smile at the camera… breathe…"

After throwing confetti at the happy couple it was time to head off for the Reception. I could now relax and enjoy the rest of this 'Special Day'.

Gillie Fisher

Market Research Manager and Secretary of Friends of Young Carers Bath & North East Somerset. Bath Rugby season ticket holder, avid cricket fan. Proud mother of two fantastic human beings, who have been a fantastic support to me throughout all the rubbish life can throw at you, but have also always been there to share in the good times, which I'm pleased to say have been a lot more frequent!

Saturday 29 May 2004

John had been chippy all morning, well for the last few weeks if I'm honest, but we all set off in my people carrier with the picnic for 16 people loaded into the back. The four of us, John, my husband, Simon and Louise, my son and daughter, were going with friends to the Zurich Premiership Final.

We caught up with the minibus that had the other 12 in it, just past Membury, and were following along quite nicely; making rude gestures through the windscreen, when suddenly John's mobile received a text message in the hand's free cradle.

I reached for it, to read out to him, but he shouted "Don't touch that!"

Well I may not be Sherlock Holmes, but it didn't take a lot of working out that something untoward was going on. He came out with a great story about one of the young girls stalking him and how he didn't want me to be upset if it was her. Sceptically, I reached for the mobile and read a very innocuous text from a young woman who he'd recently employed. He'd invited her to stay the night with us on her first day at the office, to welcome her to the town and her job, so I'd met her once.

Finally, at Bracknell, at the service station by the fire station, the minibus stopped for petrol. John and I both got out of the car too, although we didn't need anything (anything at all, as it turned out), and it all came out. He'd been having an affair with her for two years and now he didn't know what he wanted long term. I told him not to throw twenty-six years away for the sake of a shag, and that we could move on from this, and we both got back into the car and drove on to Twickenham behind the minibus.

We parked in the Stoop car park and I laid out the picnic, John was laughing and joking and drinking a glass of wine, I looked like someone had died. We walked around Twickenham thrashing it all out, and he said even if he couldn't be with Gail, who had apparently left her husband a fortnight earlier, he didn't want to be with me any more. He then suggested we go in and watch the match. I told him I couldn't, the kids were in a terrible state, it was obvious to everyone something terrible had happened.

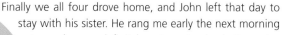

Finally we all four drove home, and John left that day to stay with his sister. He rang me early the next morning to say he was definitely not coming back. Every day for the next ten days I spoke to him on the phone and asked him if he wanted to change his mind. I started divorce proceedings on the eleventh day, and have completely rebuilt my life.

Seven years to the day, on Saturday 28th May, it will be the Aviva Premiership Final, but none of us will be there this year, even if Bath are playing, as my son, Simon, is getting married. Can't wait!

Kathy Hobson

Married, business woman, dog owner and walker, love cooking and knitting 'little people' for friends, learner bee-keeper.

My 'Perfect Day'!

Perhaps I could indulge myself and share with you what would be my 'perfect day'. I'd better tell you about me to start. I'm 57, married, no children. I do have a little dog called Alfie who I adore and let him 'rule' my life!!!

My day would start with a cup of coffee and some toast with home made jam, made by me from plums, apples or pears grown on the allotment I help to care for. I would sit in my garden enjoying the sunshine and listening to the birds singing.

I have my own accountancy business, with my husband, and I would go to the office for an hour or so. Work done I can now go home and really start my 'perfect day'. Taking Alfie for a walk would be a great start.

Over the last couple of years I have read articles about bee keeping. I felt this was something I would like to get involved with. Luckily a friend's father keeps bees and suitably clothed I went to see his hives – I got hooked (and stung a few times). I'm now learning all I can, attending courses, taking exams to hopefully have my own bees in a year or so. I am hoping to make lots of different things using wax and honey. I have made lip balm and candles so far. So my morning would be used up visiting my bees and making products.

Lunch would also be eaten in the garden – perhaps I could start eating some of that chutney I made! Early afternoon would have to be spent gardening at the allotment. How great it is to pick fruit and vegetables, cook them and eat them in one day.

I have only had one real hobby in my life so far, singing, and although I perform a couple of times a month in the evenings perhaps I could visit a residential home and sing to (and hopefully with) them in the afternoon of my 'perfect day'.

The rest of the afternoon could be spent cooking, with my friend Terri. We could catch up on our news and cook a fantastic meal for our 'other halves'. We both love trying out new recipes. A visit to the theatre to see a show, play or a comedian with friends is also a must in my 'perfect day'.

I've started knitting again, something I used to do as a child. I started just over a year ago by knitting a Father Christmas and a Snowman. I progressed to clowns (2ft tall ones!) and have made one for most of my friends and family – a cook, a one man band, a gardener, a traveller just to name a few. Now all my friends and family have one I make them and other toys for charity fundraising. That's for the rest of evening of my 'perfect day'.

Bedtime and I reflect on my 'perfect day' – have I achieved what I wanted? I have to say that if I could spend days like this I would not want for anything more – although I might be very tired!

Not what I expected

NOT WHAT I EXPECTED!

Sally-Anne Jenkins

58 years (and still with a sense of perspective) moved from Battle to East Sussex, married to Peter for 36 years.

Location, Location, Location

We had been searching for our dream home intermittently for around three years. All in all we had fallen for three or four at different times but were unable to proceed with a purchase as we had failed to entice a new purchaser for our present home in the required time. Despite some very understanding vendors, some had been willing to stall further viewers for up to a month.

Eventually we had a keen couple view, they really fell for our home, they had friends in the village who they wanted to be near. Unbelievably at this stage we were without a house we were desperate to secure a purchase on and determined not to lose the sale.

We viewed in earnest with a house style in mind, when BINGO we walked through the gate of a beautiful stone conversion of a Poor House we were stunned: golden stone, slate roof, an annexe in the perfect walled garden. We were shown into a huge kitchen with Gothic windows where I was just blown away to find a walk-in larder to complete the dream place to prepare sumptuous meals. So much excitement ensued with our second offer being accepted followed by plans being made with removal companies, finally everything was organised and we looked forward to the big day.

We packed our boxes whilst thinking of the next time we would be looking at these objects and belongings… could hardly wait.

We rose early on moving day and kept busy making tea and snacks for the moving team, a quick lunch at the local pub and then we were on our way. Just over an hour's drive to find our beautiful home waiting for our arrival… yes this was it!! First thing for me was to fill the walk-in pantry with jars of spices, chutneys, jams and all manner of dried fruits to pretend Mrs Beeton had arrived.

We had spent hours and hours measuring and planning where our furniture would be placed so it was an easy job moving in apart from the weight of every item!

Eventually we had to give in to tiredness and decided to head for bed looking forward to a night of blissful slumber. I closed my eyes only to open them again to investigate the source of the 'fairground lights' and loud crashes and thuds. Shock horror, the road to the front of our 'dream home' was heavily ladened with equally heavily ladened trucks rushing to their destinations, thundering over the uneven road surface. It was a grim moment indeed and within a split second I knew that I would begin the search all over again starting in the morning, this time remembering the wise words LOCATION LOCATION LOCATION.

Jane Carter

Live in Swansea, lover of cocker spaniels. Jewellery maker.
Business owner – Beady Eyes

Contented

Morning! Sorry, I can't talk to you just yet: I need coffee, quite a lot of it and a few cigarettes before I can get going. "Down, you daft dog, down. Yes, ok, I love you, kiss, kiss". I nip off to the quiet of my office and check my emails.

A couple of nice orders came in last night, jewellery sets. I like making those. Did I tell you that's what I do now for a living? I make wedding jewellery and tiaras and sell them through my website. It's simply the best job in the world.

I didn't think it would turn out this way, that I'd ever be this contented again and have this peace of mind. If you'd asked me fifteen years ago I'd have told you that I couldn't be happy again, not while one of my children was suffering.

I'll make that jewellery now and concentrate on getting it just so. It will empty my mind. As I work, a few emails come in with brides wanting advice on what to buy, or how long it will take to make. I answer the emails and then the phone rings. Oh dear, it's someone wanting to sell me something I don't want to buy again.

My mind drifts back to when I was twenty, my life stretching out ahead of me and I expected the future to continue in much the same way as the past – just being alive, trucking along in a carefree kind of way. We left university, got married, settled into our farm and had two beautiful kids. Years later my boy became seriously ill. I would have coped better if it had been a physical illness I think.

I'd better go onto my website and do a bit of SEO. I find this quite boring. I set up the website talking to my brides but apparently that's not good enough. I have to talk to the search engines, too, or my brides will never find me!

The day draws to a close and its peaceful here as I accept again that I have no control over any of the big things in life. All I can do is my best with the little things and so that's what I'll do again tomorrow! Goodnight, sweet dreams.

Dr. Rosa Matheson

Romany, wife, mother (and happy in-law), granny, sister, aunty, foster-mother to twenty Nepale children, friend, historian, author, always a feminist. Live in Wiltshire but still a Londoner at heart.

The Adventure

Like many women these days I lead multiple 'lives' (like the t-shirt advert!) in seemingly totally different worlds. The difficulty is which 'life' or 'world' to write about.

Should I write about my biggest achievement – four wonderful children – doctor, nursing sister and two teachers – all doing fantastic things to make this a better, fairer world? They'd probably die of embarrassment. Perhaps a day in the mantle of adoring 'granny'; I fear I would gush too much and bore people silly.

Maybe I should write about my 'railway world' where I am definitely a 'woman in a man's world' as I am one of just a handful of women who have had their railway books published. Mine have been happily successful in 'railway book' terms (not talking J K Rowling here) so give special satisfaction, particularly as one male publisher laughed at me as he told me "women and the Great Western Railway – that would never sell!" Not only did it sell, it sold out and went into reprint! That said, it has to be owned that none could have be written without my railway friends, mostly men but also some lovely ladies who generously shared their unique knowledge and experiences with me over the years.

Maybe it is more appropriate to write about what took me to Nepal in the first place – Health Partnership Nepal – (and created the possibility for this book) as it undoubtedly has changed my life.

My son then a medical student at St.George's Hospital, London had, with fellow students, set up a Medical Mission to 'hill' (mountains to you and me) villages and wanted his dad as an extra pair of medical hands. "If you're going I'm definitely going", I said, causing great family consternation and worry to my husband, as I had just recently, sort-of, recovered from a road traffic accident. My son stressed how basic, primitive, hard and demanding it would be, just to be sure we were in no doubt that we were not 'going on holiday', whilst my youngest daughter added – "it'll be hard core Mum, even for young people!' worrying my husband even more. The night before we left I was trained-up to be the 'eye doctor' doing eye tests based on the letter E (you hold up three fingers in different directions and they mimic it) and was given fifteen kilos of glasses to label up!

The village of Chokadee was in the middle of nowhere but rich with resources… it had *two* communal taps – one in the school grounds and one at the bottom of the village! It was a learning curve right from the start when tired and hungry on our first night, we staggered in pitch darkness down to the village 'café' for some dinner only to find everywhere shut up and bedded down at 6.00pm; (the village rises and opens early – at 4 a.m. we discovered.) There was a school which served several villages and had 'shifts' for the children. HPN shared the teachers' and staff one squat toilet – twenty eight of them and twelve of us – just about bearable until the water supply broke down and one could not throw water down to clear it! Very character forming as my son drily remarked.

Our patients also came from the surrounding villages, walking many hours, sometimes carrying the elderly on their backs, to then have to stand squashed in the queue crowd, in the sun, without food or water, for many hours. We started early, worked until we couldn't see for lack of light, and had only a short break for lunch, yet somehow the queues never got smaller. I had the best job of all as the results were instantaneous and the smiles on being able to 'see' were rich reward indeed. It was a humbling experience and I will never regard a pair of glasses so casually again. Don't ever throw your glasses away, but give them to be recycled to where they will change people's lives.

Undoubtedly Nepal was not what I had expected (although I am not really sure what that was) and neither had I expected what would happen after – this book, and the adoption of an orphanage!

Heather Redington

Previous NHS worker now psychotherapist in private practice. Have a special interest in trauma and am an accredited AIT practitioner and trainer. I also teach Heart Rhythm Meditation which is rooted in the Sufi tradition.

"Tell me, what is it you plan to do with your one wild and precious life?" *Mary Oliver*
"The only blessing is the consciousness of blessing." *HIK*

I used to work for the NHS. Every day I went in to my office, read emails, replied to emails, wrote notes, went to meetings and saw patients. As I saw fewer and fewer patients and did more and more admin, I realised that my heart was no longer in my work. I was drying up inside and I needed to move on.

Now I have left. Instead of going on a visit to Australia or a world trip, I am seeing the world through my encounters as a volunteer with visitors to a drop-in centre for refugees and asylum seekers. I never know what will be required of me when I go but for me this is a pleasure.

Each day up to twenty visitors come to the Harbour, which is sited in an old church hall in a side street of Swindon. It is a shabby friendly place with a few computers, a large coffee table on which is a bowl of fruit and a plate of biscuits. It is run by a small staff both paid and voluntary.

Some visitors come to meet up with fellow exiles. The air is lively with voices speaking Arabic or Eritrean or Anharic or Farsi. Others sit hunched over the computers. Many come looking strained and desperate, clutching packages of official documents.Some have had their asylum application turned down; others have to leave their accommodation. One of the lucky ones, granted 'leave to remain' is desperate to find work. She is well motivated, intelligent, willing to try her hand at anything but can't get any work. She is beginning to lose heart.

I spend forty minutes holding on a call to Immigration and then I am cut off. The young woman by my side is smiling, patient and unsurprised, appreciative whilst I seethe with impatience and indignation at the labyrinthine and inhumane system that our visitors contend with daily.

Often the stories are heart breaking. A woman from a war torn country in Africa has learned that her sons there are about to be forced to join the army. She knows this will brutalise them and expose them to the risk of AIDS. She can do nothing to help them. And I can do nothing to help her. If her husband was alive..if she had money… if ,if, if.

Two young men from the Middle East turn up as we are closing. They have started a football club for young men to give them something to do and want to know how they might get hold of goal posts.

At the end of the day (the centre can only afford to stay open for three hours a day) we say goodbye to our visitors, shut down the computers and then do the admin. I tick boxes to indicate the nature of the queries I have dealt with that day and I go home.

I am reminded to be thankful that I have a house, food and a warm bed and can sleep in the knowledge that my children and my family are safe. This is a rare privilege.

Hanna-Gael Darney

32. Born Abu Dhabi, UAE but have been living in Bristol since 2001. Nurse. Married to a brave and inspirational man, and mother to a mischievous, excitable bundle of fun known as Evan.

Just the Best NYE!

"This is not what I expected!" My two friends and I said this many, many times on our trip but the first was on New Year's Eve 2005-2006. We had set off on a trip to Mexico, Honduras, Belize, El Salvador and Guatemala to celebrate graduating as nurses and to have a break and an experience before throwing ourselves into the grinding slog of nursing in the NHS. We'd done some research to feed our excitement and had loosely planned a route. Each of us had stuff we wanted to do but were open to suggestions. My personal travelling experience has taught me that some of the best moments happen when you deviate from the plan.

Our deviations began at the start of this trip! We had planned to celebrate NYE in Cancun but when we got there it was not how we had imagined it. We didn't feel like we were in Mexico. It felt more like America. The buildings were too big and flash despite the damage caused by the recent hurricane. Fortunately, a string of happy chances, which didn't feel so happy at the time… a flight changed by the flight company without informing us, an almost missed connection (picture three girls sprinting through an airport, hair flying, muttering the odd swear word, not being able to sit together on the flight)….led to my meeting Izaak and

Aidan, two friendly Mexican lads on the plane. They were so genuinely friendly and unsleazy that it didn't seem strange to take their number. They were heading down the coast with some friends to stay in Izaak's dad's holiday apartment. They invited us to join them but we had planned to party in Cancun. Our disappointment with Cancun meant we called Izaak and asked if the invitation still stood. Sadly for them, the apartment had been ruined by the hurricane. They were staying in a room belonging to a family friend which they didn't think we'd like. We told them we weren't fussy and made plans to meet up with them.

Trying to recognise two lads in the dark that I'd met briefly in a very sleep deprived state was a challenge but I managed it. The room was in real downtown Mexico. We had to squeeze through a tall broken fence to get in. It was one smallish room with a basic bathroom with a door off its hinges. Out of respect, they leaned it over the door-shaped hole when using the toilet. The surrounding buildings in the dusty street were boarded up or had walls missing. There were stray dogs and cars on bricks. The other two boys were lovely, so welcoming. Whilst exploring the neighbourhood we came across a church with a very lively musical service going on. We had fun joining in at the back for a while. This was what we had come to experience.

We shared drinks and got to know each other. It turned out we had a lot in common. Izaak spoke great English with an American accent and we muddled through with his translation skills and our attempts at Mexican Spanish and their attempts at English. One of the boys was incredibly camp and very excited to have girls around to help him choose which shoes, shirt and fragrance to wear out that evening. He showed us pictures he had taken of men at the beach and went into a spin when he heard Madonna and Kylie. Strangely and sadly though, he was not openly gay with his friends. God knows how it wasn't obvious to them!

We drank tequila and danced the night away at a swanky bar with beds on the beach. It was a brilliant night. Back at the room, one of the lads slept in a hammock and another on a bench outside so that we could sleep on their inflatable mattresses. They were such gentlemen. We're still in touch through the wonders of email and Facebook and they know they are very welcome to stay with me any time they are in England. We didn't plan to party in that town or stay in that room with those lads but it was the possibly the best NYE I've had….so far!

Dr. Helen Sweet

Research Associate at the Wellcome Unit for the History of Medicine, University of Oxford. Researched and taught in Africa over last twelve years. Published works in Women's History and Healthcare in Britain. Married with two children and one grandchild.

Stranded in Paradise

My visits to South Africa had arisen more by chance than by design, but this time in April 2010, on my eleventh visit, I had been there for six wonderful weeks. Four of those weeks had been spent with a close friend and colleague researching a fascinating example of social medicine in rural KwaZulu Natal. I had travelled to the beautiful Drakensburg mountains with her, visited remote farms and interviewed 'isangomas' (traditional healers) in their mud and thatch rondavels with freshly cow-dunged floors. The work had been an unprecedented success and the experience, one to look back on with numerous happy memories. We had made new friends and visited old ones.

My husband had joined me for the final fortnight and we had happy spent hours transfixed as we watched a pair of cheetah cubs playing with their mother in a game reserve under the African sun. Another time we had been caught in a never-to-be-forgotten ferocious hail and thunder storm in which we'd been forced to shelter, battered, soaked and a little shaken in some deserted huts accompanied by our 'rugged ranger' sipping G&Ts with hail stones as ice cubes! On the beautiful South 'Hibiscus' Coast we had re-charged our batteries, swimming, diving and exploring the area. The four days spent in Cape Town had just flown by.

Bags were packed and we were saying a fond farewell to our beautiful view of Camp's Bay, when our hosts called up to us to switch the television on as there was important news that might concern us! In Iceland a volcano with the unpronounceable name of Eyjafjallajökull, had erupted, spewing plumes of ash into the atmosphere – maybe our flight would be cancelled? We checked with the airport – no, we would be fine, we were told! We kept the TV on and rang again several hours later – still nothing to suggest we wouldn't get home, but by the time we reached the airport the situation had changed completely and we were told "maybe in two weeks"!

Our lovely guest house owners took us back in with typical South African hospitality and kindness, thrusting a drink into our hands and telling us we could stay a further week with them and maybe things might change. Friends, family and work colleagues were contacted and, like Fagin, we began reviewing the situation! We were going to miss a friend's son's wedding – we could only apologize and toast the happy couple from a distance of almost

6000 miles south of London with South African bubbly! I had an Open University tutorial to give – that had to be rescheduled, but I was amazed by the understanding and concern expressed by colleagues and students alike. Apparently I wasn't the only tutor stuck abroad, and anyway wasn't it the home of distance learning?! I could mark their assignments online, couldn't I?

The view from our room as the sun set orange then pink across the ocean, turning the 'Apostles' of Table Mountain a series of beautiful hues, was quite breath-taking that evening. Yet the call of home – children and grandchildren – was remarkably strong, and the media was suggesting the ash cloud could strand us where we were for considerably longer than first anticipated. Would I miss my father's 99th birthday having promised him I would be home in good time? What should I be doing to prepare for my daughter's wedding in just a few weeks? Her answer was that the best – indeed the only thing to do, was to make the most of the opportunities presented to us, but to realise that once home we would be 'grounded'!

After a good night's sleep the realization finally dawned upon us that we were trapped for the foreseeable future in Paradise! The variety and unexpected nature of my work is why I love what I'm doing but this is not quite what I had expected!

Teresa Jayne Barnes

34, recently married to Steve Barnes, have three children.
Living in Hinckley for last five years.

"Dad!"

It's 14:00hrs and the heavens open, not a slight pitter-patter but a proper downpour where you will get tremendously drenched if you step outside for even a single second type of rain. Great! We're already running late; my Dad is emptying the dishwasher whilst I pace up and down the hallway swishing the train of my dress around. The wedding car has taken the bridesmaids and my Mum to the church and I know it will be another ten minutes before it returns. Then suddeny I get the urge. The urge to go to the toilet, immediately. Normally this would not be a problem but right now it is a huge problem because I'm wearing a tight fitted fishtail wedding dress.

"DAD!"

"Yes love."

"Need to go to the toilet."

"Go to the toilet then."

"I can't without your help."

Silence. In fact, a very long silence.

"DAD!"

"Teresa, can't you hold it?"

"Dad, the ceremony is going to last forty five minutes then I've got photos, then travelling to the reception. It's going to be at least two hours before I can go again."

"Oh right… err… you'd better go then."

From my Dad's lack of enthusiasm I realise I have to undertake this task alone. I enter the bathroom and look at the toilet for what seems a considerable length of time.

Right, hmmm… How am I going to do this?

I carefully manoeuvre to the white porcelain throne and try lifting my skirt, layers of netting, lob my chapel length veil across the floor and try to pull down my knickers.

"DAD, you are going to have to help me."

"What?"

It's very clear my father's usual nature of being helpful has vanished. You cannot imagine how embarrassed both of us are, nevertheless I have got a bladder screaming to be emptied and to hell with dignity. I realise my Dad is going to do anything to get out of this but unfortunately he is the only person here so he is just going to have to help. I take a more firm stance and then order (scream at) him to "get into the bathroom!"

"Right I'll hold the dress up and you're going to have to pull down my knickers."

At this point my Dad is now completely horrified. There is no way of squirming out of this one, he has got to partake in watching me have a wee. Somehow I manage to straddle the toilet whilst my Dad is buried underneath layers of silk and netting. Once I have finished doing my business I stand up and it soon becomes apparent I am unable to pull my knickers back up. So there I am, stood semi-naked with my ivory silk knickers around my ankles draped over my shoes with my Dad's facial expressions clearly stating *Get me out of here!*

"Sorry Dad but I need you to pull my pants up for me, I can't reach them because the boning in my dress stops me from bending down."

"You are joking aren't you?"

"Nope sorry Dad."

Never did I imagine or expect this – that at thirty-four I would still need my Dad to help me with my knickers!

Lucinda Frankel

Member of 'Mum's the Word' writing group. I first started writing at eighteen years old, just for enjoyment and some sort of release. This has continued through my life. I like to write about things I have experienced personally. Adoption issues are close to my heart and so are my children. I have recently discovered that my grandfather Harold Frankel also wrote poetry, but sadly I never got to meet him.

Adoption

Miranda, Lucinda and Libby
Lucinda, who is Lucinda?
Lucinda is me.
I know Libby, my daughter, Libby is me,
Very like me people do say.
Miranda my birth mum, I love her naturally,
Lucinda, Miranda and Libby.
Libby is very like me, people do say,
Does she really share my traits?
Miranda is dead, Lucinda found out,
She is a spirit, a saint to me.
Lucinda feels her
Remembers her scent from a child.
Then someone breathed another scent to Lucinda
It choked and suffocated her.
Instead she cuddled soft toys, clutching, all the time
Would not talk to people and loved animals
Hid herself away, covered her body.
As adults we did not meet
I do not know why.
My fault? I do not know why.
Miranda was a brave considerate soul, creative,
Much like Lucinda, almost her
Lucinda found out.
Libby is part of Lucinda, Lucinda is part of Miranda
Lucinda is Miranda's baby, she so bravely gave up

After that Lucinda did not want to grow up
Something crushed inside Lucinda
Two spirits lost, missed, confused, floating at the wrong times of life.
Lucinda sees Miranda every day, day in, day out, morning and night, until the limits of time.
That is spiritual
That is the gift Miranda gave to Lucinda when she left her.
Miranda never knew of Libby
This is sadness
There was only one time when Miranda, Lucinda and Libby were all alive,
It was the short time before Miranda died.
The year Libby was born, year 2000
That is spiritual,
Since then there have been three stars in the sky
Miranda, Lucinda and Libby,
One day we will meet and touch each other in the sky, in space and time,
Then we will have spiritual peace together
With peace forever,
Miranda, Lucinda and Libby.

Going Back

I remember where I was born,
I went back.
This place was somehow familiar, the woods, the trees, the smells,
it brought back memories.
Do we remember that far?
I was only a baby when there, and yet,
There is something so familiar,
I don't quite know what.
I have a deep sense of longing a yearning,
To find out,
To go back in time.
Heal the wounds I have,
Fill the missing gaps.
And yet,
I don't think I ever can.
How do I deal with that?

Kathryn (Kathy) Thomas

Born 1953, Single, 'New Homes' Sales Negotiator, passionate Harrier.

"Ever Heard of Hashing, Dear?"

At the start of this century I was seduced by a new leisure pursuit which has become an absolute favourite. All over the world diverse groups of runners and walkers gather together on a regular basis to follow a coded flour trail – with a few red herrings thrown in – laid by a volunteer 'hare'. In the UK these trails, which start from different pubs, are about 6-7 miles for runners and 3-4 miles for walkers, all returning for refreshments at about the same time. This utterly glorious activity is known as a 'Hash' (the origin being a tale in itself), and my group is The Kennet Valley Hash House Harriers.

We meet every second Sunday at 11.00am in all weathers, and there's a fabulous fancy dress hash on Boxing Day too. Milestone dates are commemorated with a special dinner or barbecue, and each mid-summer an even grander hash takes place further afield, with games to follow. Last year the trail was laid on the South Wales coast; this year it's Dublin. Leading this motley crew is a Grand Old Master (or Mistress) who works incredibly hard to make our pursuit fascinating (and not trivial).

Each hash is marked by a 'magazine' and what better way to glimpse our beguiling world than to read two of my own – you will get an idea of the full spectrum of hash conditions, and sense that the overriding feeling after a hash (any hash – no matter how tough, muddy or wet) is absolute joy!

Hash 299: 26th April 2009 *The Rose & Crown, Ashbury, Wiltshire*

Sometimes it's right to remind ourselves what a magical landscape we live in, and Vivien and John (hash novices no longer) hit just the right note with their marvellous trail today, laid with both cheerful enthusiasm and precision – walkers and runners returning to the pub in synchronised contentment (no mean feat!). Very well done, and our heartfelt thanks to you both.

When I awoke this morning I just knew it was going to be one of those splendid hash days – there was a thin mist, the air was still, and then the sky cleared to a piercing blue with the occasional cotton-wool cloud, and a gentle breeze started up – bliss.

A lovely mixed crowd – including a growing 'family' of assorted dogs – gathered at the pub, and the walkers got ready in record time (after checking their emergency supplies for the umpteenth time:- tissues, pain-killers, fruit, keys, mobile, sweets, more tissues, lozenges… and loo paper!). Then we were off, swept up to the top of the Ridgeway in a tide of idle gossip and chit-chat, pausing in awe on several occasions to appreciate spectacular views of glacial valleys, long barrows, fantastic tree lines and – as we descended – more pastoral, idyllic scenes dotted with cows, ponies, smallholdings, woodlands… and an almost hidden lake.

As usual, the walkers (unlike the poor, save-your-breath runners) chatted about a huge variety of subjects from Annie & Kevin's 'bellissimo' holiday in Italy, and the wonderful Easter weekend 'bunkhouse' break enjoyed by Liz & Robin, to how the economic slump is even affecting employment at local schools, as well as causing real unease at the likes of Honda (not to mention scribe's attempts to sell new houses!).

But somehow, up there nearer the clouds on such a glorious day, you felt just a little bit more able to cope with whatever life throws at you. I know I did. The bar staff were cheerful and efficient, the drinks were reasonably priced too, and I returned home in a better mood than I started – the hallmark of a perfect hash.

The joy of the hash is that they are all so different. Here's a 'flavour' of another one:

Hash 311 – 11th October 2009 *The Bolingbroke Arms, Hook, Nr Wootton Bassett, Wiltshire*

Well, they say the sun always shines on the righteous… so what did we do so wrong today? I checked the weather forecast before going to bed on Saturday night and it advised a mild, bright and dry Sunday, with the possibility of light drizzle later on… so I confidently ventured forth in 'appropriate' clothing and not a little attention to my hair. Big mistake. HUGE!

Sadly, the small, select, stalwart throng which actually turned up (though several of our missing members were – to be fair – 'enjoying' the half-marathon instead) will need no reminding that it poured. And poured. And poured. Despite coats, hoods, and – in my case – an umbrella as well, we were soaked through several layers right down to our underwear, and our feet squelched in our boots. And that was before we'd even got half-way. And it's only the beginning of October!

However, we encountered some delightful cottages on the first part of the trail, and were sorely tempted by the 'Cadbury's chocolate farm', but we gamely soldiered on into the woods and fields with some dodgy stiles, and even dodgier puddles. I had it on good authority that we should even have seen some deer… but I suspect they'd found some secret dry shelter and weren't letting on!

Well, folks, there's not a lot more I can say, other than to express my absolute delight at arriving home to change into dry clothes… the lot I was wearing went straight into the washing machine, even my 'wash and wear' walking boots… There's steam everywhere, even as I type… and it's now long into the evening! But, hey, don't the hard slog, the fresh air and the martyrdom make you feel smug?

See! They say variety is the spice of life so upwards and onwards, and, as always, our grateful thanks to our intrepid 'hares'.

Rev. Rosemary Franklin

I was born in Gloucestershire the youngest of four children, my father farmed. We were a churchgoing family and my parents were involved with the work of the church and the village life. After school I trained as a Norland Nanny and then travelled in the Far East and retrained as a secretary. After I married we lived for two years in Singapore and then returned to the UK. I have three children — my daughters are both married and my son is not. I have one granddaughter.

Me – a Priest!

It was with great surprise that I found myself being called to be a Priest. My calling was gradual until the final when a series of events propelled me to talk to my Priest and he encouraged me to take the next steps. At the time I was the Diocesan President of the Mothers' Union, a worldwide organisation that promotes Christian Family Life. I spent the whole of the time when I and others were exploring my calling expecting them to say "no thanks you are too old". There is an expectation that you will be under fifty and I was over this.

I found myself in the classroom three weeks after I learnt I had been accepted for training. The whole of the two years passed very quickly and it was only with God's grace and help that I got through. It was a challenge! Running the Mothers' Union in the Diocese; at that time there were nearly three thousand members; attending meetings in London and throughout the country and being back at 'school' after so many years as I was never an academic.

I now work as an Assistant Priest in the Parish of Cirencester which consists of three churches. My day starts at 8.30 with Morning Prayer, with my colleagues, said in the Catherine Chapel of the Parish Church which is a peaceful and wonderful way to start. This is followed by a Staff meeting one day, or taking the Assembly in one of the church schools. A quick visit to the Parish Office to pick up any messages and then pastoral visiting which may be taking Communion to a Housebound Parishioner, or the Tuesday communion service in the Hospital. Home for lunch and then the preschool service or meeting in the Cornerstone Shop with mums whose children are at school. My day may include a Funeral visit where I meet the bereaved family and plan the service with them. In the evening there is often a meeting sometimes in one of the surrounding villages, sometimes in one of the Parish rooms.

It is a job that I love and one that is full of surprises, laughter and tears. It is difficult to describe one day as each day is different and the variety enriching. For me it is the interaction with the people of God that I enjoy from those nearing their end on this world to the very young starting out on their journey. The immense privilege of being alongside people in their moments of joy, sadness and helplessness. Moments at home are often taken up with preparing services, talks and reading to stay up to date with the current theological thinking. I find my new 'job' immensely satisfying, but it is not one I ever expected.

Laura Kennedy

24. Work and live in London with my partner Henry.
Amateur photographer and seamstress (basically I couldn't paint or draw
if my life depended on it but I can follow instructions).

Inspiration

Rain. Shine. Sunset Sunrise. Parks. Roads. Cold. Hot. Short. Long. Aching. Invigorated. Calm. Thoughtful. Determined. Inspired. Sweaty. Happy. Exhausted... all words that I associate with one of my favourite past times, running.

Until two years ago I was resigned to the fact that I was not one to exercise, I did not stick to any attempt at a gym routine, nor could I run for one kilometre. Since then I have run a half marathon, am training for another and have set my sights on running a full marathon

My inspiration to begin running came when living in New Zealand, where I worked as an Emergency Medical Dispatcher. It was my role to answer 111 calls (our 999) and talk people through first aid and life saving procedures. Whilst this work was incredibly rewarding I began to feel that the emotional aspects of the role, coupled with being far from home, away from oldest and best friends and working unsociable hours began to take its toll. These factors pushed me to do something for myself which gave me the clarity of mind, fitness and personal satisfaction to re-build an emotional and physical balance (the scenery wasn't bad either).

When I returned to the UK I was worried that I would loose the habit and stop running, however the reverse happened, out of paranoia I signed up to a half marathon which meant that my training increased and I run further and longer in the UK than I had ever run in NZ. Long distance running takes you to a whole new level in which you are so tired that it is impossible to think about the daily stresses that you hold and all of your energy is focused on making it home and not tripping over tree roots. What I like is you can run anywhere, for any length, at any time and with any one. All you need is you (and some decent trainers).

Two years on from beginning to run and I continue to run as regularly as I can, fitting it into my routines as much as possible. I've had some set backs with the odd injury which is to be expected and have recovered with the aid of patience and strengthening exercises. I've realised that as part of living our lives things will continually be sent to try us from all spheres of our lifestyles and that it is so important that we identify things that strengthen us as individuals. For me, the answer is running. It helps me to tackle these challenges, clear my mind and provides motivation in the best and worst of times.

Most people who do not run and do not see themselves as 'runners' dismiss it as I did for a long time, mainly from the fear of not being able to run any length of distance. All I can say is give it a go, you'll be surprised (as I was) at how quickly you can overcome these barriers and the sense of reward is definitely worth the effort.

Minding my own business

MINDING MY OWN BUSINESS

Kelly Scully

From Bicester, Oxford. Business woman and jewellery maker.

Finding my Own Business

When I fell ill in 2005, I really didn't think it would present me with an opportunity that could quite literally change my life. I was fortunate that my illness was not long term so my health continued to improve over time but whilst I was waiting for my body to repair itself, I was very bored. I was restricted in what I could and couldn't do so was pretty much confined to the sofa or bed and, other than television and reading, there was not a lot else I could do and I was beginning to feel very down.

It was not long after I was released from hospital that my elderly neighbour took me out to get some groceries. On the way back from the grocery store, we passed a large craft shop and I mentioned I used to make jewellery as a child. She suggested that given my current situation, I should perhaps take it up again so we went into the shop. I bought some basic materials and when I got home began making earrings, necklaces and bracelets.

As friends and neighbours came to visit me, they each fell in love with the pieces I'd made and one by one, they were being sold to them. It was becoming a little cottage industry and I was finding myself becoming more and more creative. After a while it dawned on me that my favourite materials tended to be pearls and crystals as I just love the sparkle they created and of course, so do brides.

It wasn't long before I made the leap from jewellery to begin making tiaras. The first ones I made were pretty basic as I was learning as I go, but within time I learnt new techniques, created my own products and started to develop my own collection of pieces. Within a couple of years, I'd made lots of tiaras and my pieces were really beginning to take on a life of their own and my company name was becoming well known.

So as the end of 2010 approaches and I look back over the past five years and think about the path that led me to where I am today. My business is growing from strength to strength and my creative vision has grown so much. My products are a regular feature in magazines and I've had my jewellery featured on the cover of one of the best selling bridal magazines in the UK. It's hard to believe that such a wonderful business could have come from a traumatic life event like my illness. I certainly didn't think it would turn out like this.

Audrey Beaumont
White Milk With That!

What is that noise? Why does my head hurt? Please don't tell me it's already 7am… I beg my husband for an extra five minutes in bed and as a response, I find myself dragged out of bed… I am up!!! With about thirty minutes to get ready, I start wishing that I'd actually done the ironing yesterday instead of just thinking about it!

Rendez Vous is a very short drive from home, Hubby drives, I tweet! I love getting to work early when no one else is around. Newspapers in one hand, cigarette in the other, I am now ready to start my day and open the doors to the unknown. Please don't start thinking that I don't know what I'm doing, it's just that once I've opened the doors, who knows who will come through them!

One of my regular customers has just told me that her husband passed away last week and I'm trying really hard to hold my tears. I've been here so long that most of them now feel like part of the family… Not the best way to start the day. She is followed by a man who is insisting on having white milk with his coffee, this time I have to make sure I don't start laughing and ask him again whether he wants hot or cold milk. "White milk please", I give up!

I really do love my job but dealing with the public isn't always easy and my lack of patience often let's me down. How am I meant to keep smiling when I don't even get a 'please' or a 'thank you' or when the answer I get to a "Good morning" is "Latte"… I normally end up giving as good as I get which I probably shouldn't but I'm a true believer that respect has to work both ways. As I say quite often – you can train your staff but you can't train your customers! Luckily most of them are absolutely lovely and they make up for the not so nice ones!

He has done it again… All I can smell is Simon's famous chocolate brownie… Why did I decide to go on a diet; a little piece won't hurt; will it?

Lunch time was pretty busy and the day went quickly but I haven't been brave enough to open the post yet. The thing about running your own business is that nothing nice ever comes in the post anymore; it's all bills, bills, bills. I've also noticed the huge pile of washing up waiting for me; definitely need that piece of brownie now!

The end of my working day has arrived and it's time to go home and even though we have seen each other all day, Hubby and I say "hello" to each other as we get in the car then Hubby drives, I tweet…

I'm really thinking about doing the ironing tonight but start with a glass of wine and remember why my head was hurting this morning!

Galia Orme

Argentian born now living in Sussex. Married for nineteen years with two lovely daughters aged fourteen and ten.

Chocolate!

I am incredibly fortunate to love what I do for a living. Not that this was always the case. I found myself three years ago, aged forty, working in a job I didn't particularly enjoy and feeling that I'd never found what I was really meant to be doing with my career. After over twenty years of working in a range of roles, from legal research to sales and marketing (mainly ones that fitted around my family life), I felt it was finally my time to dedicate myself to what I love in life. So the challenge was to find something that I genuinely love doing and am actually good at. My two main passions have always been music and chocolate. Having sung in a band for several years, I knew this wasn't something I would be able to make a real career out of, so I concentrated on my love of chocolate. I didn't even have to look very hard; the idea for my business came to me suddenly after trying raw chocolates that a friend of mine made for me. I was amazed by how easy it is to make and how pure and delicious the chocolates tasted. After spending several months making raw chocolate myself and perfecting the recipes, I developed raw chocolate making kits with all the ingredients and recipes so that anyone can make these amazing chocolates themselves. By the summer of 2008 I had set up my company CHOC Chick (I figured that since I could no longer really be a Rock Chick, I could at least be a CHOC Chick!) and was trading online.

So what's a day in the life of a CHOC Chick like? Since I'm also a wife and mother of two lovely daughters, my days are pretty full on. I wake up at 7am when my eldest daughter Maia gets up for school. I make coffee and chat with her as she gets ready and generally tidy the kitchen, put the washing on, fold some clothes and try and get as much housework as I can done. Once Maia sets off for school at 7:45, I then go and wake my youngest daughter Ella up.

125

We chat as she gets ready, have breakfast together, feed the dogs and then set off for school.

I'm back by 9:00am when I grab another coffee and start my work day. I have a small office at home and spend most of the morning answering and sending emails, organising online orders, speaking to buyers, writing marketing information, updating my website and dealing with any supply/delivery issues that normally crop up. I take a half hour break at 1:00pm for lunch, try and walk the dogs and then am back in my office till 3:30pm when Ella comes home from school. We usually have a snack together and a chat and I usually continue working until 5:00pm when Maia comes home and I start thinking about making dinner. Some afternoons the girls have 'clubs' or 'classes' which means this afternoon I have enough time to make a chocolate truffles mix which I need for an event I'm doing at the weekend.

My husband Bill works till late (normally home at 8:30pm), so the girls and I have dinner together, tidy up the kitchen and then settle in front of the telly for the rest of the evening. As the truffles mix has now set, I end up making chocolate truffles in front of the telly while watching an amazing programme about dissecting a giant squid (doesn't get stranger than that really!). Bedtime for Ella is around 9:30pm. I love reading to her and we still enjoy reading at least one of her old children's books each night. We have a cuddle in bed and at 10:00pm it's time to say good night to Maia. Bill and I spend the rest of the evening on our own chatting about our day and I'm usually in bed by 11:30pm.

Mary Marsh

Born in Malvern 1963. Happy to mess about in dad's woodwork shop from early age. Studied Environmental Biology in London and stayed to work for an environmental charity. Financial difficulties of the charity inspired me to become a Chartered Accountant and fifteen years later I became 'freelance' — very liberating. Now a self-employed furniture maker — the clever bit will be making a living from it!

Sublime Alchemy

As a chartered accountant I used to mind other people's businesses but what I really wanted to do was work with wood and mind my own. In 2005 the opportunity arose for me to make that change and I grabbed it with both hands.

My motivation was four-fold:

1 I wanted to leave some trace of my existence. In the world of accounting much of your work is shredded after six years and you're left wondering what all that effort was for.

2 I wanted to do something for which I actually have an aptitude. I was a good accountant but I'm a much better furniture maker.

3 I didn't want to leave it until I was too old to have a go or just plain dead.

4 The one thing worse than failure is regret.

Being an accountant is handy, of course, when you're running your own business. Except that in this case I should certainly have advised myself not to give up a sensible and successful career in accountancy for the uncertainty of life as a craftsman. But there is more to life than job, house and mortgage. I know I should be planning for my old age and worrying about my pension and I do worry but not enough to miss this opportunity. Too many friends have died long before they got anywhere near retirement age. This life is short and it may be all there is.

There is another way of looking at the idea of minding one's own business and it's particularly relevant to the craftsman. There is something about working with your hands which necessitates a very fundamental minding of one's own business. In order to get the wood to do what you need it to do; to get each joint to fit perfectly; to plane the drawer down so that it just glides into the cabinet with a hair's breadth to spare; to sand the surfaces evenly until they feel like silk and then take off the sharp edges just enough that they're softened but still crisp; all this requires that you shut out everything around you and focus your mind, your eyes and your hands on the wood and the tool which you're using to shape it. If you're tired or distracted then it probably won't go well and it's better to leave it until later or tomorrow when you can give it your undivided attention.

If this sounds spiritual then that's because when it all comes together and you get it right, it is spiritual. It's no coincidence that the Shaker motto was "hands to work; hearts to God" and that the rule of St Benedict contains the words "laborare est orare" – to work is to pray. There is a sublime alchemy between wood, craftsman and some higher power that creates the beautiful fusion of craftsmanship and timber which at its best is pure magic.

Lisa Cooney

38, born in London, lived in Surrey since the age of three. Married to Richard with two gorgeous daughters called Lili (7) and Daisy (3). Worked in retail for the first half of my career and then moved into recruitment and training. In 2006 we built our own house. I wanted to be able to buy beautiful things in 'my style' in one place, without having to drive around all over the place or pay multiple amounts of postage and from this came the idea for 'Out of Love'

A Family Affair!

I have lots of ideas almost on a daily basis for ventures that I think will make life easier, better or more efficient. Most of these ideas stay as just that, mostly because of time or money (or both). Whilst building my house though I had an idea and enough 'things' came together that I thought 'I could really do this'.

I wanted to be able to buy lovely things for my new home but could not get them in the homogenised High Streets that we seem to have developed. I found myself having to drive to far-flung villages to find independent retailers who are still supplying beautiful but different offerings to the market place. However, I had a small child and was pregnant and driving all over the South East was not my idea of fun. I shop regularly on the internet and even more so since having children. "I need a website where I could get all my lovely things, pay one lot of postage and save myself all this running around" were my thoughts.

Although I am described as a Mumpreneur and the site is mine and all the day to day running of the business is down to me, there is NO WAY that I could do it without the fabulous family that I have around me. I mentioned that we built our own house but I did not say that it was right next door to my Mum and Dad so the little people are quite often to be found 'next door' when I am up to my eyeballs in photography, bookwork, orders etc, etc.

My very talented cousin is an illustrator, graphic designer and web developer so I knew that we could definitely build a website that worked but had the feel that I wanted. This sounds easy but there are lots of technical people out there who have no artistic ability and vice versa so it is fabulous to find someone who can do both (and well).

My mother has been in the Interiors, design and wholesale industry for more years than she would care to remember so without really thinking about it I had lots of Industry contacts that I could utilise to find stock and suppliers. In the end it almost seemed daft not to give it a go.

That is not to say that it has not been hard work and I am often found still working at 2am to upload images or stock take. As well as the website it is nice to get out and about to meet people and let them see the stock up close so I also do lots of Summer fetes, Christmas markets and Home Soirees. This involves choosing stock, loading up the car, setting up, selling, greeting, as well as packing up, unloading the car at the other end.

The only way to make it work with the family is to be very strict about the times that I work, hence working late into the night. I try to have the time that the children are at home free. The whole point was to have a business that worked around my family and not the other way round. A balance that was very tricky at first but I SEEM to have found some kind of balance.

It is a balance though that could not be achieved without the support of my husband (having to change days off and holidays around Out of Love), my parents and their never-ending support. Good job they love spending time with their grandchildren and my cousin who would love to be enjoying more of his idyllic life in France but cannot because of all my interruptions.

In short, although I am 'minding my own business', it really is 'a family affair' and I would not have it any other way.

Alice Perret

Age 37. Live at home with my Mum and younger brother and sister. Studied Agricultural Engineering at Plymouth University and Psychology & Sociology at the University of Wales. Spent some time working in Camphill Communities (life sharing communities where people with or without learning disabilities live and work together) here and in the US.

Cats and Drums!

My typical day starts at 6am with my cat Hernia hopping onto my pillow for a cuddle. I love him dearly, but wish he would choose a slightly later time to wake me up. The first thing I do in the morning, after banging my head on the beam above my bed, is to check that all five cats (Hernia, Baby, Ollie, Nancy, Squeak) are present and correct, and that they are fed and watered.

We have only had Broadband Internet Connection for a few months and it is still a novelty to switch on the computer and not have to hear that awful screeching sound of dial up. The computer (an antique, well almost) gets fired up and then it's time to start the time consuming task of checking e-mails. As I work from home, it is not uncommon for me to still be in my pyjamas late morning.

I run a not for profit company called Omanye offering African drumming to adults (16+) who have learning disabilities. We offer African drumming and other workshops to schools, community groups, festivals etc. up and down the U.K. I spend a large chunk of my time responding to requests for Omanye to either perform or offer workshops. I am also responsible for maintaining the website and updating it when necessary. Presently, a lot of my time is taken up writing funding bids.

How I started drumming… A few years ago I used to take my mother to drumming classes and I would wait outside in the car. After a few week the teacher came out and asked me to come in and join the class, a few more weeks later and I took the plunge and went and joined the class. The rest, they say, is history!!

Djembes (drums) are neither small nor particularly light, and, if we have a workshop or evening class, then there is plenty of lifting and shifting to be done. It takes almost half-an-hour to load the van with all the drums and paraphernalia that we need. Most days my time is spent either in front of the computer or behind the steering wheel.

African drumming is something that will take a lifetime to learn, there is always a new rhythm or parts of rhythms to learn and techniques to master. I don't really have a favourite rhythm… there are too many to choose from. Every new rhythm becomes a favourite, until you hear the next one!!! My motto is 'have drums – will travel' and boy, do we travel… Halesowen, Liverpool, Buckingham, Suffolk, Oxford, are a few of the places we visit.

Free evenings are usually spent at home with the family either watching television, reading a good book or talking. Most nights before I got to sleep I watch a few minutes of 'The Waltons', it always sends me off to sleep. The perfect way to end a day!

Life-long learning

LIFE-LONG LEARNING

Fran Risbrook

Born 1936 Hawera, Taranaki, New Zealand, now long time resident of Southampton. Retired teacher: always loved my work. Grandmother of three lovely grandchildren

Teaching the Teacher

As my husband and I breakfast comfortably together, in our house in Southampton listening to the morning news, one would have hoped we were feeling calm. Not so! As usual, our blood pressure rises as we hear accusations of incompetence made against our teaching colleagues. How the 'uniquely challenging' situations in some 21st century schools are not being competently met. How 'schools in poorer areas, where the problem is most acute' are being failed. We wish the critics had actually taught – few have!

"Systematic, synthetic phonics" aggressively declaims the expert, "Without these skills no child can learn to read", but experience has shown me that children have their own thoughts about how they will learn. I remember my first teaching post in New Zealand. The mistakes I made. I remember Kiri!

"Nah!" The word spat out. "Nah", snapped the child, tossing the book onto the table. "Nah! Just only pictures. No words."

Astonished, I looked at Kiri. Her flat, brown nose, nostrils encrusted with yellow mucus; matted hair with ominous white specks adhering to the strands; the ragged dress, beneath which bare feet, the toenails wedged with dirt, protruded, were an unappealing sight. At five years old the small girl was no beauty. But the brown eyes, indignantly meeting mine, were bright and determined.

"Come to school learn to read. Nah look pictures!"

The latest, beautifully illustrated, initial reading scheme, designed for the 'language deprived' child, aimed to encourage discussion of everyday scenes, thus helping the development of vocabulary in the 'emergent reader'. The books had no printed text and it was this that had aroused Kiri's ire. She had come to school to learn to read not look at baby books. Learn to read she did. The rapidity of her progress, proof of the intelligence behind those bright eyes.

So, Miss Collins, the new Infant Mistress of a small, country school in New Zealand, also began to learn. In this case, not to equate cleanliness with intelligence. I certainly learned a lot at Wetaweta Primary School.

In those days, fifty years ago, children started school on their fifth birthday. Their initial shyness didn't last long. One day, whilst I worked with other groups, two little new boys, Tama and Heke, ventured out to the play area beyond the open doorway, just outside my classroom. All were happy and busy. Suddenly, deafening bangs thudded onto the corrugated iron roof. Outside, petrified, stood Tama and Heke as large stones and clods of earth rained down from the sky. Inside, the children sat in frozen silence. A silence broken by hideous screams as the terrified infants rushed into the room, bee-lined for me and scrambled up my skirt and body to hide their faces on my shoulders. They were shaking with fear. Still, the others were mute, sitting like statues.

I sat down with the little ones on my lap and we waited, quietly, for the explanation of this attack – a school governor, one of the local farmers, had decided to blast tree stumps from the school driveway, not told the Head Master, and got the explosive spectacularly wrong! Tama and Heke were greatly impressed, "Wah, dey throw stones at yer, dem teachers?" they asked their big sisters. I often witnessed this still, alert, silent reaction of Maori children when they were faced with an unknown experience. A reaction to emulate, I feel!

Recently, Sam, my eleven year old grandson told me proudly of the apple crumble he had made at school. Nowadays, it is the expectation that men, also, need to learn to cook. Quite right, too, but it wasn't always so. Fifty years ago, only girls attended Domestic Science lessons.

I remember it was fun to see the girls from Wetaweta School returning from Cookery, carrying their pie dishes of tasty food and surrounded by cajoling boys. "Hey, come on, Hine, what did you make? Just show us. We won't touch it", but the girls maintained their dignified air, tossing back their long, black hair and casting fierce glances at any lad coming within grabbing distance. Those cheeky boys tried many persuasive tactics but the girls were too wise for them! A lesson here for all women today, I think!

Even after years of teaching and living in England, now, forty-seven years later, I still think, with respect and affection, of the fine children I was privileged to teach. Perhaps the modern 21st Century educationalists should remember how much we teachers can learn from our pupils.

Iainthe Matheson

25, daughter of inspirational parents Rosa and Ian, sister to the most amazing brother and sisters, aunty to the most perfect little one, friend, teacher and lover of life.

My First Class

Walking into my classroom I feel an immediate sense of purpose mixed with contentment and satisfaction. On the drive here I may not have been particularly looking forward to work, but now here, I feel happy and lucky to be standing in this room with the day that is ahead of me.

I did not get to this point directly; it has taken years of decision changing, worrying and confusion, mixed with a few years of travelling which, admittedly, helped take the edge off the time. In the end it has been the support, encouragement and love of my family that has got me here. Now I stand in this room, a space which I and my class have created together, which has housed many memorable times which will stay with me for many years if not forever.

My first class. The first group of children who have been entrusted to me for their early steps in educational, emotional and social development. A scary but yet wonderful and exciting prospect. My aim, to instil in them an excitement towards all forms of learning and to ensure a sense of belonging and trust was grown between us. This has allowed me to support them in many different ways, which consequently has rewarded me in ways that are beyond words. To be the person who a child in fear and need comes to for help, to be the one to bring a smile to a tearful or worried face, to watch the small steps entwine together to become huge achievements; from counting to 10 or 20 or 1000 to learning to tie ones shoelaces or cut up their own dinner. To see the joy and light in their eyes with each new experience be it having remembered to put their tails under the line or having had the chance to visit the seaside or simply to spend time just reading a book one to one. These times may sound contrived or petty but to me having only one in a day would make that day one to remember. Rarely is there only one such occasion in a day, a teaching day is so varied and full of such times it is one of those rare careers where you can honestly say no day is the same. That is not to say there are not times that are not so good, indeed this year has been an emotional roller coaster of deep downs but extreme highs; for me and for some of the children. We have, however, come out together nearing the end of this year stronger than we started and more prepared and ready to face the next steps, whatever they may be.

Helen Curtis

I was born in London and after qualifying as a teacher moved to Surrey where I met my husband. We moved to Highworth when we married 26 years ago. We have a son and a daughter

My Day

On a Wednesday and Thursday I work as an Advisor for Specific Learning Difficulties / Dyslexia. The role is very varied with no two days being the same.

My day begins with the alarm clock at 06.20. After a shower, a bowl of cereal and a cup of tea I'm ready for my first school visit of the day.

I'm going into discuss strategies to help a Year 5 boy record his ideas. He has some great ideas but always writes them in a continuous string of letters without leaving spaces between the words and uses lower and uppercase letters inconsistently.

I suggest that his page is marked into a grid so that he can write one word into each space. This makes it much easier for him to read it back. I draw a highlighted line onto the writing line and demonstrate the correct formation and size of letters. He has a go writing on the line and is successful. He comments that, "the magic line is great!" This is one part of my role I really enjoy, where I can suggest some very simple strategies that have an immediate impact.

My next visit is a teacher training session to demonstrate Precision Teaching. This technique enables children to build a sight vocabulary which helps them to read. The session goes well and it is great to hear the teachers saying that they can't wait to get started with their class.

I used to be fairly nervous when training adults but I am gaining confidence now and don't lose too much sleep when I'm preparing to deliver training courses for both teachers and their assistants.

I return to my base, lunch comprises a quick sandwich while I check emails.

The last visit is to a Y6 pupil, he will be leaving Primary School soon and is still having difficulty with his spellings. I produce my little bag of plastic letters and start to assess his ability to say and blend the sounds in words. He works hard and I give him praise. I'm struck by his honesty as he admits that he doesn't always try hard in class as he finds writing difficult and often gets into trouble. I rummage in my bag and show him a postcard of a snow scene. He likes the picture so I turn over the card to reveal that it is painted by a mouth painter, an artist without the use of his hands. We talk about all the things he's good at and likes doing. I enjoy being able to take time with the children to try to build their self esteem and help them to overcome the barriers to their learning by exploring with them the best way to learn.

In the remaining hour and a half I have to write my 'Record of Visits' for the day and prepare for the following day, as usual I work over my hours!

I return home to the smell of fish and chips. My daughter has got in before me and has cooked tea. A quick tea and change and I'm ready for my art class, I'll be late again but I insist on going every week. It gives me a chance to unwind, catch-up with the other ladies and when we've finished chatting, we do some painting!

Dr. Diane Drummond

Lecturer and researcher. Historian. Published author.

Academia is Fun

My day starts as most of my days, with one of our two cats mewing and scratching, wanting their breakfast. I need to respond to the cats immediately this morning as I teach at 9am and have to have everything up and running in the teaching room before that. So it's feed the cats, come back upstairs to kiss my husband of thirty years awake, have a shower, blow-dry my hair – badly, downstairs to tip down breakfast and off to work.

The first two hour session today is comparatively easy, which is relief as I teach on the Master of Art programme on Thursday evening until 9pm so being in the class room less than twelve hours later can be a shock. I'm with a group who are in their final year of their honours degrees at the university I lecture in. It's the first week of a new semester and we are watching a feature film on Bloody Sunday, Northern Ireland 30th January, 1972.

Researching the causes and events of that day will be our focus for the rest of the year. The film is violent, shocking and deeply upsetting, drawn from eyewitness accounts. The events remains controversial even after the publication of the Saville Report in the summer of 2010. For students, most of whom are approximately twenty-one years old, terrorism in Northern Ireland, 'The Troubles', seem disturbing but distant, difficult to comprehend. To me, at my age, it's still raw and recent. Being aware of the emotions involved in seeing such a film and being thoughtful about student reaction is important.

The next session is shorter and much less strenuous, pleasant and friendly with some good and interesting exchange with students. Then I have a long meeting with a group of students who are carrying out a research project, oral history interviews, for an event to be held on International Women's Day on the 8th March. This year's topic is 'Pathways to Decent Work for Women'. After discussion the working title for our event is 'Jobs for the Girls?'

The group have already decided who they will interview for the oral history project – women of different age groups in education and nursing, together with those who've had little education or opportunity. Most of their interviewees will be relatives, mothers and grandmothers. One student lives in South Yorkshire, another comes from east London. It is clear that they are the first generation of women in their family to have decent access to education. They plan to carryout a vox pop of young women of their own age, to see how they feel about current prospects and the future for women. We discuss this. Everyone in the group is very gloomy about their own futures, given the current recession and colossal public spending cuts. I ask if they feel that they have fewer opportunities than I did in the 1970s–80s. They all say yes.

Perhaps their interviews will put their own experiences into a different perspective. Perhaps they won't and shouldn't given the situation we're facing in higher education. One of the delights of my job is seeing people, of whatever age, developing their thinking, understanding, confidence and independence. It is an especially positive experience when I see this happen to students who have been held back by their backgrounds and circumstances, something we get a lot of in my university where many students come from the working-class and ethnic minorities. I wonder how much longer I will continue to teach such individuals given government policies now being introduced.

I spend lunchtime with colleagues in the café in the university entrance. One of the benefits of working here is spending time with colleagues, friends since I have worked at the university for so long. They are witty, know so much and are very, very talented. Even in a small, new university, more known for its teaching and widening participation than research, I'm in the company of authors of many academic books, novelists and poets. This place is certainly no 'ivory tower', there's too much varied teaching for it to be that, but one colleague has had three books published in a fortnight!

My first two jobs this afternoon are supervising final year students doing dissertations. They have just submitted reports on their research to date and are planning twenty minute presentations that will be marked in two weeks' time. The subjects that our students decide to research can be very diverse. Listening to students' ideas and arguments and responding with key questions is challenging and often exhilarating. One student is investigating the results of aerial bombing on civilian morale in Britain during the Second World War. The other a rather obscure performance art/rock group that have been operating in the Balkans since the 1980s. The group might be totally obscure but they throw up some interesting questions about 'the state' and how it might function in a better world. In reaction to the terrible recent history of this area of Europe this group dream of a 'virtual', international state, even peace, in a stateless world. This takes me to the very edge of my knowledge and experience, but is interesting and thrilling.

The rest of my working day consists of preparing for a session to be held first thing the next day and doing some marking, online. Like so many people today much of my work is on the computer. Whether it is showing students visual evidence such as films, digitalized books, newspapers, newsreel film and historical documents in teaching sessions, setting up intranet materials for student or marking, I do it on the computer.

Today I'd like to do something else on the computer, write. I've tons of research to carry out and write up. My research is currently on railways in the British Empire. Last month I went to India to give two papers on the subject. This was very exciting and interesting as I had the opportunity to travel on Indian trains including the lovely Kalka-Shimla Mountain railway as I went to a workshop at the Indian Advanced Studies Institute that is housed in the former Viceregal Lodge in Shimla. I'd love to sit and write, but am too tired after teaching last night, so it's home to feed those cats again and spend time with my husband.

Jenna Broadway

25. (Loving) Daughter. (Inspirational) Teacher. (Dedicated) Friend.

A Good Day

Brrring. Brrring. Snooze. Brrring. Brrring. Snooze. Friday, one more snooze.

Brrring. Brrring. Off. Haul myself up. Rub eyes. Turn on light. Look at the sleeping guy still snoring. Sigh.

Dressing room. Look hazily at clothes. Pick outfit. Which necklace? No time for shower. Quick wash. Brush teeth.

Turn on grill. Crumpet in. Kettle on.

Pour pellets. Clean water. Open the Hatch. CLUCK CLUCK CLUCK. Big cheesy grin. Check for eggs. Clean poop.

Butter breakfast. Coffee in flask. Curtains open. 7.45 out.

Chris Moyles. Lots of traffic. Busy car park.

Reception. Corridor. Stairs. A12. Emails. Set up.

Morning Ma'am! Morning Ma'am! Hustle before school. Lesson 1. Registers. Ma'am. Ma'am. Ma'am. Where is this. Where are those. Success stories. Amazing smiles.

Break. (Detentions.) Coffee. Cake. Set up.

Registers. Homework. Excuses. Tidying. Success stories. Smiles. Frowns.

Lunch. Quick phone check. Emails. Lunch (if lucky). Dinner queue squabbles.

Registers. Homework. Excuses. Tidying. Success stories. Some smiles. Frowns. Excitement.

3pm. Sighs and smiles all round. Dedicated students in. Amazing work evolving. Sink scrubbing time. Paintbrush sorting. Glue lid search. Marking. Planning. Meetings. Assessment. Stack chairs. Pick up pencils. Procrastinate. Internet distractions. Daydream about holidays. Positive phone calls. Negative phone calls. Rewards. Reports.

Home time. Computer off. Lights off. Sunglasses on. Diversion. Pub. Quick drink with work friends. Giggle. Another drink. Smiles. Laughter. Reflecting. Planning.

Proper home time. No cars. No boyfriend. Let girlies out. Feed them. Collect eggs. Wash hands. Ring parents. Relive highs and lows all round. Plan Sunday lunch. Have shower. Get dolled up. Hair done. Straight or curly? Shiny lips. New perfume. Boy returns. Quick chat. Smiles. Cheeky kiss. Scrounge a lift. Off to my girls.

Sun shining. BBQ on. Designated chef. Mistake. Burnt burgers. Undercooked chicken. Crisps and dips. Laughing. Wine poured. Wii out. Game on. Shrieking. Chocolate devoured. Round Two. Wine poured. Music cranked up. More Wii. Winners. Losers in denial. Round Three planned. Taxis home.

Shock at the clock. Shoes strewn anywhere. Into bed. Snuggle up. Good day.

Oona Matheson

Teacher, loves singing and dancing.

Decisions

Driving home with tears in my eyes, struggling to see through the tears I can't help but question whether I have made the right decision. Today was my last day teaching at my first school. I had started work there straight after university and had found it a huge challenge, a steep learning curve and a very long working day. The school is in a very challenging area of my hometown and as a result teachers there have concerns over and above the daily tasks of planning, teaching, marking, meetings etc.

My second year in the school presented my biggest professional challenge to date, teaching and supporting a child who was going through the most awful turbulence in her home life. Throughout the year she was moved to six different foster homes and had a failed return to her birth parents. Naturally, due to all this change and turmoil, she rebelled in both her home life and school life. I knew the key to being there for her lay within a strong positive relationship, which I initially found a real struggle to establish but, as time passed, after many tears, hers and mine, we managed to build a mutual understanding, I adjusted my expectations and she endeavoured to meet them.

By the end of the academic year I had grown very fond of this child and all the others in my class. However I was soon to leave, not just the school but the country. I had accepted a teaching post in Dubai, UAE and would be leaving in just a few weeks. I had made the decision five months earlier and it had not been an easy one. If I decided to move I would be leaving not only my school, the children that I really cared for and the friends I had made in the fantastic staff there, but also my family; my partner of six years, my parents, sisters and brother and my newly born nephew. I had never even holidayed in Dubai or the United Arab Emirates, all I knew of the country was what my parents had fondly described from their memories of living in the neighbouring Abu Dhabi thirty years ago and what I had learnt from my research on the internet. Nevertheless I had made it my intention long ago to travel the world and experience as many cultures and changes as I could. I believe that is how you grow as a person and knew that this job offer was the perfect opportunity for me to begin a new journey.

Trying to keep the reasons for my decision in my mind I drove away from the place where I had started what I hope will be a lifelong career, where I had learnt so much in such a short time, where I had worked so hard to establish myself as the kind of teacher I would want to be seen as. I absolutely loved my time working as a teacher in this school and although I'm incredibly nervous about moving to an unknown country, with a new home, new people and a new school, I am so excited and feel so lucky to be doing what I love wherever I am in the world.

140

Joyce Owen

76. Retired Teacher. Married to Peter. Lives in Swindon. World traveller.

Thoughts of a Retired Teacher

I retired from Primary Education in 1991 after enjoying nearly 40 years of service. Since then I am fortunate to be part of a retired group of couples (not all teachers) with whom I have enjoyed 'World Wide Travel'.

Inevitably we have visited many schools in many countries and have always been aware of the quality of dedicated teachers and of pupils who are eager to learn. On one occasion in Shanghi we visited an 'after school academy for gifted children' and were amazed to find parents sitting in and observing the lesson from the side of the classroom. When the teacher was not satisfied with a student's performance and results, he merely reported to dad and enlisted his aid to rectify the situation. This exercise took place during the lesson, much to the embarrassment of pupil and dad. Was this another dimension to the policy of 'Parent's Involvement in Schools'?

In Alice Springs (Australia) we saw what surely must be the original programme of 'Distance Learning'. This an example of modern technology meeting the needs of children scattered over vast territories. I understand that they used to do this via radio links, but today it is more productive through major technological advances such as Skype.

Thailand provided me with the opportunity to demonstrate my teaching ability when invited to take the class by the Principal. Although conditions were somewhat primitive, it was a joy to teach and talk to such friendly faces. The children demonstrated their command of English by their responses when I talked about schools and children in England.

In Singapore I met up with one of my former pupils who was teaching there. Sarah informed me that she was about to embark on her first date with an American Navy Officer. Both my husband and I reverted to the role of surrogate parents issuing her with warning about 'all manner of things'. I am happy to say she married her American Officer and is happy settled in Colorado with three wonderful children.

All these wonderful experiences emphasise the educational theory that 'Education is not the arrival at the destination, but it is the journey getting there.' Little did I know when I left education in the 20th Century, I would be still be enjoying it so much in the 21st. It shows that learning is a life-long activity, particularly with three grandchildren in school, and a daughter and son-in-law who are head teachers in Swindon.

I've lived a lot
in my time

I'VE LIVED A LOT IN MY TIME!

Margaret Goodrum

Mother of three including twins, grandmother. Long-time resident of Liverpool, always been a 'sewer' patchwork maker.

A Life in Threads

Looking back from my now sixty-year old perspective it seemed to start with stitching bits of fabric together to make a whole – be it something for a favourite doll or teddy to wear and decorate a naked form, at about ten years of age.

Going on to washing tutus up to my armpits in soap suds, cutting off and replacing ribbons, cords and buttons: to and from dry cleaners, I found myself in a humble wardrobe position at the Royal Opera House, Covent Garden. This dizzy height was reached via GCE Needlework and a Bespoke Tailoring and Pattern Cutting course at the London College of Fashion. All was to be dumped after a short foray into the world of touring as wardrobe mistress of the Yogi Bear Show. This £75,000 spectacular featured Huckleberry Hound, Boo Boo and Yogi Bear as my companions en route around the U.K. I was often to be found letting out tight costumes and replacing more fastenings along the road. Sundays and Mondays were usually taken up with dry cleaner or launderette visits somewhere between Aberdeen and Oxford, with a fat purse of coins for the machines.

Then it was head down into teaching and playing with notions of Piaget; threads of dreams and Bettelheim; and some consolidation of number on the way. Old money got changed into new. The Initial Teaching Alphabet meant every teaching resource had to be duplicated and we weren't even helping children to become bi-lingual. And not forgetting 'Play with a Purpose' and child-centred learning. In the early 70s, as a newly qualified teacher working in an inner-city London primary school, I was thrown in to the deep end of team teaching, integrated days, topic based learning, whilst working in an open-plan, family grouped environment. It felt like free-fall, a bit noisy and messy at times but full of enthusiasm and potential for all staff and children alike.

Twenty years later I found myself supporting some poorly spelt survivors of one such experiment in early years education, whilst working as a Basic Skills Literacy Tutor. From Hertfordshire to Merseyside they fell under the promised spell of 'instant writers and readers' to become badly spelt adults.

But once having 'felt the fabric' it was never to be forgotten – oh! the market stalls of Dewsbury and Leeds where off-cuts of denim by the pound could be obtained. Later, oddments acquired got made into a Jacob's coat of many colours for children pleased to wear something new – never mind the lack of colour co-ordination or today's mantra of matching outfits.

Then in the 21st Century in the mid-fifties of my life when adult-education offered a new horizon: I lay down on my yoga-mat one night, for exercise and relaxation surrounded by a patchwork kaleidoscope of hanging quilts. The opportunistic luxury of signing up to learn a new skill and develop a latent interest was grasped. It was great to be propelled back into the world of 'feeling the fabric'. This time it was colour and printed dyes or design in cottons and silks rather than the pattern and dyes in worsted weaves, cavalry twill and herringbones of the tailoring world that held my fascination. There was a subtle difference and it had new terminology too – like fat quarters, and making Mary's Triangle or Wild Geese, sliced out like butter with a cutter's wheel. And it's back to imperial measures using fractions of inches and leaving metric out in the cold. It involves collecting volumes of fabric bits and then slicing them up into tiny shapes to re-assemble them into a design. Out of this activity is produced an everlasting quilt for a much loved daughter or friend. All this is done not alone: colour consultations are required and friends, husband and daughters get drawn in. Fabrics are brought back from trips abroad by family members and returned to them sliced up and re-worked as quilts, hangings or cushions with embroidery, buttons and photographs added. The life in threads happily continues in the new decade sewing many life experiences together.

Margaret Bacon

Live in Wiltshire. Lover of literature. Author of seventeen books.

Gardens!

I have a love/hate relationship with my acre garden. No, hate is too strong a word. When, at the end of months of toiling in it, I sweep up the last of the autumn leaves at the end of November and tell it that I'm leaving it to look after itself, the relief I feel is akin to that of a weary mother as she settles a much loved but exhausting infant down for the night. Yet at the first hint of spring, at that magical moment when the sky brightens, the birds begin to sing and the gardens demands attention, I answer its call as instinctively as any mother responds to the call of her child.

I didn't ask to have a gardening obsession any more than I asked to have a writing obsession. I think the compulsion to write was probably born in me, but the gardening obsession developed over the years. It started when at the age of twenty-two, with an interesting but ill-paid job, an inheritance of £800 and in need of a home, I bought a one-up, one-down cottage at an auction for £750. It had mud on the floor, sagging ceilings, no electricity and an outside loo tenanted by frogs. Access to this property was to be had by climbing over a low stone wall, a condition of the sale being that a gated entrance should be made. Then I had to make a path to get from the gate to the cottage. A local farmer obliging dumped his unwanted bricks over my low wall and I spent long evenings laying down a path which undulated with the bumps in the ground, leaving some bricks sticking up much higher than others, but I was proud of my first incursion into landscape gardening.

Two years later I was deeply offended when a chance acquaintance leant over my gate and commented that my path was more spirit than level, but he could re-lay it in a weekend. Let him try, I thought. It's not as easy as it looks.

I kept my distance as he removed my bricks, dug foundations, put sticks at various points with string between them, kept checking levels, generally behaving as if he were building an arterial road rather than a cottage path. Then it was finished and I saw that it was good; the bricks were laid in a pattern, like a woven carpet, it was level, it was lovely.

He was a Civil Engineer. I married him.

Civil Engineers are nomads, they build a harbour or a dam and move on to the next job. So we moved from place to place making gardens. The most challenging of these gardens was the one in Guyana: it was the only garden for which we had to provide our own soil. The natural ground was mud baked hard by the sun, on which nothing grew except a kind of creeping grass.

This home-made soil was precious so we planted our hibiscus, bougainvilleas, oleanders and plumbago in oil drums cut in two and punctured with drainage holes. Vegetables were more difficult; they had to be grown in raised beds made out of planks of wood called callaloo which came in various shapes and sizes. I found the climate physically punishing, but the impatient gardener in me rejoiced in the way everything grew so quickly; green shoots would appear in days and flowers within a few weeks. It was irresistible; we acquired more and more oil drums, mixed up increasing quantities of soil. The soil recipe was simple; one third sand, one third palm fibre and one third donkey dung. We collected the palm fibre and sand in a van. The dung was delivered on a cart, the productive donkey being led by a ten-year old boy called Basdeo.

The donkey dung had other applications; it was used to repair wooden tubs if they sprang a leak, acting like plastic wood. Soon after we arrived an old East Indian woman came to the door offering milk from a big wooden tub.

"Look, no cockroaches," she said stirring with her hand.

I looked at the not very clean hand, I remembered what I had been told about wooden tubs and donkey dung, and I explained that we didn't drink milk in our tea. This was true since we had stopped doing so when we had found there was no other supply of milk to be had apart from the sweet condensed variety in tins.

That habit of two years became permanent and there is no milk in the mug of tepid tea that sits alongside me as I write this all these years later. I sit at my desk remembering, trying not to think about all the things that need doing in my unruly acre garden, but I know it will win. It always does.

Carolyn Crawley

44 but don't particularly care. Born in Southampton, lived in Singapore, Buckie, Thurso, Kingston on Spey, Rafford and Aberdeen before I was eighteen, Ruislip, Compton Bassett, Swindon and Highworth since (seventeen years). Happily married — we have camped for seventeen years and never once argued over pitching/decamping the tent. We still miss each other whenever we go back to work afterwards. Have two lovely daughters, great family and friends. Life is good, Simple things are the purest pleasures.

Today My Procrastination.

I hide in books. Not in a jump out and 'boo' kind of way but more in the sense of hiding from the world around me. Not that there is anything to hide from far from it, it's just the older I get, I'm coming to the realisation that I'm using my love of books to avoid...stuff. We have routine and lots of time for love and all the necessary day-to-day 'stuff' of sharing a life with a husband and daughter (sometimes plural) but dull stuff doesn't get much of a look in. So much better to sit on the sofa and share a book than to tidy or polish or know for sure that I haven't got much money in my bank account. But then there is other stuff to half-do like running a Brownie pack and being district commissioner (sort of), and of course work, and college, and planning things to do elsewhere – the best of which is camping, with husband and daughter and books.

I get genuinely excited when collecting the latest book from the library by my favourite author. I am annoying, laughing out loud and reading out loud anything that tickles and ranting at the things that outrage me when reading the occasional newspaper.

I grew up in a small Scottish village or to be more accurate several different Scottish villages and small towns, there was no daytime television or often anything to do at all and, in retrospect, a fairly dysfunctional family. My sister was, and is, a normal sister which meant we hated each other then and love each other now but our mother had a then undiagnosed chronic heart condition. Our dad was a good dad. He taught me to sail a dingy despite working unbelievably long hours off shore, went to night school (not college) and filled in any gaps mending/cleaning cars and taking us food shopping. I think mums then just cleaned and cooked but I only really remember mine sleeping when she was ill and hairdressing when she wasn't, and talking to me about the world. She did care intensely about our education and I remember her being so proud of my reading and even once about a poem 'wot I wrote'. She loved us and life fiercely. She died when I was fourteen and my sister was just ten, in her sleep, while our dad was away thankfully not on an oil platform but far enough away, too far away, in Aberdeen. It is hard not to let something like that define your life. If you find yourself recounting why you live your life the way you do because of an event or trauma or injustice or wrong doing, ask yourself is it not bad enough to suffer a trauma or a circumstance but then to let it rule your life? In the western world we generally have choices. It took me years to realise that I am still me and responsible for actions I choose,

There is some remarkable Banksy art that encapsulates it all but then I love Banksy. I feel in it my youth which I missed in part. Not in the way of those destined to a lifetime of poverty – I have an excellent education and free mind to save me from that – but I didn't just grow up at 14. I'd also had many years caring and cleaning and worrying just so much about everything before then. My passport photo at the age of 15 was that of an old woman. Getting married at the age of eighteen to someone on the rebound and moving hundreds of miles away from everything I knew was definitely not smart. Life is sweet I have seventeen fabulous years, and counting, with my funny gorgeous husband and my beautiful eldest daughter now twenty-one (step-daughter in truth) and with my wonderful youngest daughter of ten, fast approaching eleven. I have a lovely if somewhat messy house and have much to keep me occupied.

But back to today, a normal day, a cuddle; a quick tidy; then off to the library for more books and then maybe we will go to the Mela in Swindon. I should be finishing my college assignments before my holiday starts properly but I can do that later. The luxury of procrastination… and education… and love of the arts… and most of all love.

Janice Knight

Winner of the 'Make It Happen Award' in 1996 and member ever since;
qualified coach, mentor and mediation practitioner.
I love helping people fulfil their potential.

Making It Happen

It is so good to be in a place where I feel happy with my life, and with what I have achieved. I am glad that my experiences and what they have taught me have enabled me to help others to overcome difficulties that they are facing. I find that very rewarding.

I am fortunate to have been given great gifts of creativity and imagination. I was born with and been able to hold on to a great joy of life, a belief that anything is possible, practical problem solving skills, a great sense of humour, and also with a good deal of common sense and being well grounded.

My skills helped me cope with becoming a mother at 18, and at 25, with four young children, I set up a small building company when my husband was diagnosed with severe depression and was unable to work. I knew virtually nothing of the building trade. We had no money, but I did have great self belief, and optimism. I typed out some cards on an old portable typewriter, saying that I could undertake minor building repairs at reasonable rates then walked the local streets posting these through letter boxes. A week later I had my first job to clearout blocked guttering and I was on my way. I enrolled in the local college to do Construction Technology and sat with 16-18 year old lads who were mainly looking to get into Quantity Surveying.

I ran the business successfully for five years until my husband was able to take the work on. By that time I employed between twelve and fifteen tradesmen and had won tenders with local builders and the local authority.

I have applied the same principles to everything I have done in life. It doesn't matter how long it takes or what I need to do to become competent. I just roll up my sleeves and get on with it.

By the time I was thirty-eight as well as having managed to raise my family, obtain formal qualifications, and be holding down a well-paid job as a manager for a Logistics Company I decided I wanted to give something to others who had not had such good fortune as me. I started with teaching adult literacy one evening a week. I continued in full time employment but devoted one or two evenings a week to teaching. From adult literacy I went on to teach interpersonal skills; coaching skills; designing and delivering courses for people with disabilities; running courses for women who wanted to run their own business and more recently courses on Conflict Management and Mediation.

I have been mentoring women in business now for over fifteen years and I organise a 'Make It Happen' award each year to identify women with potential and offer them support. In my spare time(!) I love dancing, socialising, drama and script writing, singing and doing anything new. I am happy with my life and what I have achieved and I just want to go on doing more new and exciting things.

Anne Fisher

Currently working in the NHS and in the home. Live with husband and two sons. Am looking forward to retirement when I can enjoy my hobbies of gardening, walking and music. Plan to pursue a new interest and learn more about 20th Century glass, ceramics and furniture and maybe be the next Fiona Bruce or even find a valuable treasure!

Moving Memories

The last ten years in my life have seen many unexpected changes. One of them was a house move, said to be one of the most stressful events in life. But it was a happy time I'm glad to say, yet it set me thinking about a house move over 50 years ago… and question when do we form our earliest memories? Do we really remember events as early as we think, or are we told stories and claim them as our own?

I have, I believe, a very clear, early memory of the day we moved house when I was not quite three years old. We had to move as I, the third child, was a girl after two boys and would need my own bedroom soon.

The layout of the old house is familiar to me still. The sitting room had a dining area with a bay window where there was an ottoman (I have it now in my own home). I would kneel on it to look out of the window and watch my brothers leave for school and then return. I was desperate to be with them, to join them at school, so much so I dressed up in their school clothes and set off in the direction they always took. I seemed to get a long way but was soon rescued by my mother. In reality I had only made it across the road to a grassed area before I was brought back.

I can also picture my parents' bedroom. I was in a cot at my mother's side of the bed. I probably stayed in a cot longer than most children would these days. I have a vivid memory of a little routine for putting the light out before I settled down. My father would tell me to blow at the light to turn it out. As if by magic, it went out. Obviously my father turned off the light at exactly the right moment but for me, he had performed a miracle. He was then and henceforth a hero and performer of great things.

Now the family were moving, though just along the street it could have been the end of the world as far as my younger brother was concerned. He was heartbroken and very worried he may be leaving his circle of friends. Maybe that created tension, but I became aware that something big was afoot. My mother tried to explain what was going to happen, the words "we shall soon be moving house" sticking in my mind. How can you move a house? A moving house sounded frightening to me, what if it fell down? I can remember sitting in the kitchen. It had a window with a high sill, being small all I was able to see was the sky. It must have been very windy as the clouds were racing along at a fair lick. At last everything fell into place and I relaxed. The clouds racing by gave the illusion we were moving. Houses really could move, we were on our way, it was so smooth and we were all safe!

Well, we left number 114 Millfield Avenue and moved the few hundred yards to number 72. Within minutes I was happy. Immediately next door there was a little girl with a doll's pram and a tricycle. We soon became firm friends. My brothers had new friends too and despite earlier fears, were still in very close proximity to their old ones. We had a big garden and I had my own bedroom, (for a while anyway till baby number four arrived!)

That house is still a big part of my life. My mother still lives there after fifty odd years. There have been many changes and improvements. The house has seen births, deaths, marriages and many a family get-together. It holds so many happy memories, some sad ones too. Maybe my memories are not all mine and they've been cobbled together by family legend. But it doesn't matter. I hope this house I live in now will generate as many memories. Stories in families are important and should be passed on to those we love.

Marion Binks

Lancashire lass, born June 1920. Married twice, two daughters, and one son. Lived in Swindon since 1965.

Yesterday today.

For some, although living in the 21st Century, they are actually inhabiting past times. One such is Marion Binks. Marion is now in her 91st year and forgetfulness has taken a hold. For Marion discussing recent events is all but impossible – her todays are her yesterdays. She lives in a time warp of her previous times and these memories are razor sharp. Some of these memories revisited each and every day she shares with her son Andrew:

My childhood was spent in Moss Colliery Road, Clifton, Manchester, and I went to St Anne's school next to the Church. My teacher was Miss Sharples who lived in the big house next to the woods, with the huge entrance gates. She was very strict and used to get her 'Paddy' up a lot, and hit you over the knuckles with a ruler. My first 'holiday', when I was about 11, was with the Brownies when we visited the Bolton Moors, some nine miles away, the furthest away from home I had ever been. We went by Charabanc (funny word that) which had an open top with a tarpaulin cover if it was to rain.

I loved helping Father on his three smallholdings. He had three because each house in our terrace was allotted one. Two of the neighbours left their plots empty and Dad took them on. He kept hens and I loved feeding them. These he would occasionally kill for the table, and he supplied eggs for many folks locally. I used to love the trip to Manchester on the tram to buy chicks at the market. Growing and picking our own vegetables, which he also sold, and germinating flowers from seed, gave me a lifelong love of gardening.

Like everyone else I left school at 14 and then got a job at Pilkington's Tiles which was situated at the other end of Clifton woods, and across the Manchester to Blackpool main line. It was a good 45 minute walk from home in all weathers. I only stayed there a while and in 1936 I got a new job. I really loved it, working in the printing and setting department with Mr Ridgeway and his boss Mr Anderson. I made lots of new friends and especially one girl Vera Wilkinson who is still my friend to this day. In the years leading up to the War we would spend many happy hours dancing at the Palais in Manchester, and going for weekends to Blackpool, staying at very low key bed and breakfast digs. I must admit that sometimes we even came back on a Monday morning and went straight to work. A couple of 'dirty stop outs' we were. Vera and I loved promenading on the local 'monkey run', where all the local lads and lasses would congregate, at nearby Pendlebury, it was such fun. One thing I never liked was walking in the Town, when all the men would hang around on street corners, near pubs etc and pass comments about pretty young girls; I did not like that at all.

Years after I married Ron [Marion was married twice] we came to Swindon in 1965. I enjoyed being a full time housewife and mum to you three. It was very satisfying. I enjoyed my gardening, cooking, baking, making jams and preserves, flower arranging, marquetry and wine making (though I couldn't drink a drop as my migraines were a constant problem) I got involved with a few local clubs, and Ron and I were in the Swindon Lions club. I particularly enjoyed serving with Eileen Ayres in the Lions Shop on a Friday afternoon. This was probably the first charity shop in Swindon and we had some fun

"Would you change anything in your life, Mum?" her son asked whilst compiling these notes?

Out of the blue came, "Yes, only one thing. I should never have given up driving lessons fifty odd years ago, after failing my test for the fourth time. The instructor told me I was a 'Bloody Fool'. Do you know what? He was right".

Joyce Murgatroyd

94, born, bred, and still lives in Swindon.
Long-time retired teacher, avid reader of history books.

Passing Fads

As a nonagenarian I have lived a lot and seen a lot in my life. My early years were greatly influenced by my grandmother who was born in 1838. Her father was a farm labourer and Sarah never went to school and so was illiterate. As a child I had to read the newspapers to her and I learnt a lot from this situation. I determined to do as well as I could when I grew up. I worked hard at my studies to become a teacher. My two daughters followed in my footsteps and became teachers too and I get some satisfaction in thinking that we have contributed something to society even today.

A year after I was married war was declared in 1939 and this had a great influence on our lives. My husband was an engineer which was a 'reserved occupation'. He was working at Dagenham when war broke out but later transferred to Swindon Great Western Railway. At this time we were stopping at my parents' house. One night we went to bed and shut the door. In the morning we could not get out as the door lock had got stuck. We had to climb out of the window and slide down the lean-to roof of the kitchen, where my father was waiting with a ladder for us to descend to earth. I remember this as both men were in a tizzy about being late for work. Punctuality was very important then. It was unheard of to be late, not so now I think as even the trains can't manage it!

The war years were traumatic yet we managed to survive, but life changed considerably as during the war housewives and mothers went out to work in the factories and offices. This left many children without any supervision after school hours, becoming 'latch-key' children. Nowadays more women go out to work through necessity or choice but there are many 'after-school' clubs and after school care.

When the war ended new eras came. We had the 'Teddy Boys', then 'Mods and Rockers', the 'Flower People' with their ideas of free love; and the 'Ton-Up' boys with their motorbikes. I'm not sure what we have nowadays apart from so-called 'celebrities' or 'wannabees' who want to be famous overnight. 'Rock and Roll' came and was very popular and the guitar became more popular than the piano, which I learnt to play when I was young and still love to play even now.

Nowadays it's all about technology with all sorts of 'pods' and 'pads'. I like my writing pad and to hand-write my letters. Mail to me is letters coming through the post-box – it doesn't come with an 'e' in front!

Looking back over my life it seems as if I have lived in two different worlds, before the war and after. Which one do I prefer? Well…!

Eileen Kettle-White
Today and Then

Today we have computers, telly, videos and DVDs
Then we had no telly or anything else to see.
Then it was skiffle groups and Rock 'n'Roll
Today it's rapping and some dance up a pole
I spent most of my teenage years on war-work in World War 2
There was no such thing as being idle, we were given jobs to do.
We had coupons to get clothes with – skirts, trousers and coats,
some made of blankets were the fashion
All food – meat, egg, cheese, tea, sugar etc., were rationed.
Then no nightlife or comfy bed
Nightime was spent in shelters instead.
We had small torches pointed down – not much light to be seen
Not much fun when you met some one and you don't know what you've got
Until you can see him in the light and realise he's not so hot!
Sometimes we all feel as if we would like to go back a few years and
Be younger than we are today
But would I like to be a teenager today?
Not blooming likely
Not these days
No way!

Lorna Dawes

Born and bred to a Great Western Railway family.
Member of the Thursday Morning Ex-Railwaymen's and Women's Club,
sometime painter and keen gardener. Precious cat owner.

Passing Times

Two years after the house was built I moved in with the help of the local midwife who carried out her rounds on a bicycle with a Gladstone bag strapped to the back. The house had been built in the corner of a field close to the Hreod Burna brook in one of six terraces. It was a peaceful world.

The world now comes to me with the inevitable increase in noise levels. A main ring road is now clearly visible within metres of the house so there is 'round the clock' traffic including emergency vehicles with sirens blaring and motor bikes with noisy 'silencers'. The street outside has the constant movement of cars and vans with the occasional security alarms sounding. Overhead there are many aircraft be it flights to the U.S.A., light aircraft and helicopters, sky diving planes and the very poignant planes repatriating the fallen servicemen to R.A.F. Lyneham; the latter always on an obvious flight-path.

The field and whole local area is now built on apart from the Recreation Ground. There are new houses at the rear and a factory trading estate beyond the ring road with an underpass in between, hence street lights stay on all night so the flowers in the garden have no period of darkness as would normally be the case. Despite all these difficulties a pair of blackbirds raised three young in the garden this year and the cock bird has already visited to decide about next year. So nature has a way to overcome problems that are a bother to humans.

The World also comes to the house by way of T.V. and radio bringing almost instant news from remote places and the telephone means I can chat away to a relative in Ohio as if we were in the room together. In this 21st century world my cat has her own supermarket, previously she relied on scraps. Now she also receives letters from her insurer and Vet addressed to her personally – 'Nipper'.

The Town itself has grown into a vast area, meaning the actual countryside seems further away, although we have some lovely parks and gorgeous countryside when reached. On the plus side there are all manner of groups and organisations catering for most tastes.

Many aspects of my life have improved over the years and I would certainly find it hard to live as we did all those years ago with just one coal fire, sash windows that had ice-patterns on the inside and no hot running water but a scary geyser lit once a week for bath night. Happily, hot water and central heating are now installed.

The things I miss are the views of the Downs from the house; the little corner-shops in each street;the tradesmen of every kind delivering to the house and giving little gifts at Christmas to say 'thank you' to their customers. I also miss the crowds of twenty or so children playing together in the street and the Salvation Army Band playing outside, at especially Christmas. I miss the quiet times in the garden with only the sound of steam trains in the distance.

There is, however, much to enjoy. The house is warm with labour saving devices at the touch of a switch and the garden is beautifully sunny on a fine day. My grandfather's favourite saying was – 'Count your blessings' – and I do.

Mair Hubband

Born Wales, lived in Highworth, Wiltshire since 1966. Recently widowed. Voluntary reporter for local community magazine.

Nothing Stays Still

On a lovely day in May 2010, following my husband's death in March, the day before what would have been our forty sixth wedding anniversary, I decided to spend a week in North Wales visiting my mother and sister. This was the first time since 2007 as my husband was unable to travel because of his illness.

Whilst there on one particular day my friend Lena, who I first met when we were students nurses, took me out on a nostalgic ride to the Lleyn Peninsular where I grew up in the 1940s and 50s.

Over the last fifty years there have been vast changes in the countryside everywhere. I found it very sad to see many of the farms and small-holdings no longer in use. Gone are the people and the animals have disappeared. Farmers have had to diversify.

The houses in the small villages are mainly second homes, where people only occupy them during weekends and holidays. The shops and the Post Offices have closed down, therefore, as people get older and can no longer drive they have moved to the towns to be near the supermarkets and other facilities.

As a child we all attended Services in the churches or chapels during the week and three times on a Sunday. It had a wonderful sense of community. This is no longer the case, and most of the buildings have been sold as a result of dwindling congregations. Today they are either houses or Art Centres!

We later visited the small seaside village of Aberderon at the end of the peninsular. It consists of white-washed cottages and has an ancient church where some of my ancestors are buried near the sea wall. We often visited the village as children and each August Bank holiday a Regatta was held. The ice-cream tasted delicious while we watched the boats. Boats trips to Berdsay Island across th bay were held during the summer months. The church on the island was founded in the 3rd century A.D. and at one time three pilgrimages to Berdsey were reckoned equal to one pilgrimage to Rome. Many of the pilgrims were buried there.

Whilst at Aberderon we met a gentleman, who was in the same form as me at school, for the first time in fifty years and later another girlfriend who I was friendly with until I moved away. It was wonderful to chat and reminisce about the 'old days' and catch up with the changes over the last half-a-century.

What this visit profoundly brought home to me is – nothing stays still, life goes on, let's grasp it. Life is not a rehearsal!

Inga Keating

Born London 1926, evacuated to Hertfordshire in World War Two. Lived and worked for one year in my grandparents' home country – Sweden. Served as a policewoman in London before marriage. Widowed eighteen years, three daughters, including twins. Eight grandchildren.

Am I Lucky?

To me my life has always been busy and interesting. After my marriage I lived in Canada for five years where I had my twins. When I returned to England I did miscellaneous secretarial work, taught typing to blind students with R.N.I.B for four years and took an Open University course gaining a B.A. degree in my fifties! By this time I had moved to Highworth where I have now lived and worked for thirty-three years

It is difficult to sort out a single day's activities except to say I am not a lover of housework; I also no longer enjoy cooking so I automatically keep things simple. There are certain enjoyable activities I undertake but not every day – Tai Chi classes on Mondays, Petanque (French Boules) every Friday and choir every other week concentrating on learning harmonies.

I am a compulsive collector of various forms and materials of owls. My first was a pale blue glass one from a factory in Sweden. I now have about eighty. I keep them all around the flat in various clusters. The latest is a doorstop comprising six stuffed owls about 8" high. There are smaller collections of teapots, model buses, fans and masses of books. I very much enjoy reading crime thrillers.

Another interest I have had for many years is drawing and painting. I have worked in watercolours and acrylics. A few years ago I took part in a course of Chinese Brush Painting which I am tempted to go back again to some time soon.

I very much enjoy my Fridays playing Petanque as, apart from giving me essential exercise, it is played outside and I meet with people I get on with very well. As a bonus my younger brother also plays. There is a light-hearted competitiveness and always much laughter.

Many of us are members of the U3A (University of the Third Age). This is an excellent organisation which works for retired people. There are many different groups covering a myriad of subjects an activities from travel, languages, painting, antiques and collectables to name a few. They occasionally organise trips out. We travelled to Newbury recently to the Watermill Theatre to see the play 'Moonlight and Magnolias'. We lunched at Hungerford.

It is a mistake to think that on retirement one will get bored – believe me there is never time. There is so much on offer. Volunteers are always needed and I have had some of my most enjoyable jobs taking part this way. For years I worked a few hours each week for Age Concern, Samaritans, the local hospice and latterly for the library delivering books to the house-bound.

I am also fortunate in having good friends who I meet regularly sharing evenings or occasionally, as with one friend, playing word games on a Sunday.

I must not forget my close family – three daughters constantly in touch and visiting when able; brothers – one of whom I see twice a week to share meals – and grandchildren, always a delight and interesting watching their development.

Yes, I am indeed lucky.

the BOOK PROJECT

---o-O-o---

When my husband and I went to Nepal on a Medical Mission with Health Partnership Nepal in the Spring of 2009, we had no idea how much it would change our lives. The images I had carried of Nepal were of big white mountains and smiley people made of tough stuff! I had heard about the Himalayas, the treks, the Sherpas and the Ghurkas but I had not heard about the grinding poverty, the deprivation, the abandoned children nor the dreadful plight of many of the women. Once there these things were hard to miss.

I have always been interested in women's issues. As a self-employed consultant I project-managed women's 'roadshows', I mentored women in their work lives, taught women's history and women's studies at university, and generally championed women's causes, so when I met a female adventure guide, Inka Trollsas, in the lounge of the small hotel in which we were staying in Kathmandu, I was fascinated by her story and moved by her project. Inka told me she was teaching young Nepale girls to become kayak instructors and that the first group of girls had been disowned by their families, so radical and unacceptable was it considered. She had to find money to house and feed them as well as money for all the training equipment. I was inspired by Inka's enthusiasm and commitment and by the young girls' determination, so, I promised to help.

It took sometime to find the 'right' way to go. We could not give any more time to 'fundraising' as we were totally involved with that for the orphanage we had adopted in Kathmandu. Then I had a 'light-bulb' moment, to create a project whereby women here would help women there simply by writing about themselves. The beauty of this simple idea was that it would not take a lot of time or work (I thought) and the end product would be a wonderful 'snapshot' of women's lives in Britain today. It would also be a fantastic historical resource for future generations.

I wrote to Inka and asked her what she thought – this was her response:

Wow! This is a fantastic idea! So, I am definitely interested, and I have so many exciting things happening here, I will be so happy to share some of them in this book! I had one of the most amazing rewarding days yesterday, starting a program for six new girls who want to become river guides in Nepal. One of the girls I started teaching two years ago is helping me to teach them. They are all of different cast from different villages and towns of Nepal, all very strong minded girls who have decided they will not live a traditional life marrying at young age and becoming a house wife. Studying further is also not interesting or possible for them – they are hoping for a very special and unusual career – female adventure guides.

We started the day by waking up at 5.30. We would then a walk / jog uphill to a small hotel who lends us their swimming-pool. Up at the beautiful setting, we did some very basic aerobics, to further train their stamina, but most of all practise coordination which was for some of them very needed practise. It was also a very fun and different physical activity for them. I then taught them to do push ups, in this field they will need to especially build up their arm muscles. For two reasons really, one being they have to get much stronger to be able to work as a kayaker and raft guide – including carrying heavy equipment. The other reason, a skinny girl is not very likely to get employed, even though she might be a good kayaker, with great attitude and good English.

After this exercise we started the swimming lesson which seemed to be their favourite. It is amazing to see how these girls, who can not swim – still enjoy the water so much! How hard they practise! I am really not a swimming instructor, and I used to be a really lousy swimmer to be honest. But since I started this project I have had to get better at it myself, and have developed ideas on how to teach swimming with help of other volunteers that have helped me from time to time. Only one of the girls could swim a little bit before today. But this morning I was sure, that in a few days time they will all be fine. They love the water and they practise and learn quickly.

After cooking together and having a good rest we picked up our club kayaks and started walking down to the lake. It was a bit hard to see how hard for them it was just to carry the kayak, but then I remembered how I myself had the same problem when I learnt!

I was really excited to get the girls on the lake. I must say I was a little bit disappointed at how difficult they found it to be, some of them taking a long time to figure out how to go forward or even how to hold the paddle. It made me really angry as well, remembering that it is this society that holds back the girls so much, that they find it very hard to learn new things. But as much as that is true, for the same reason, they still manage to learn quickly as they get the chance!

It took a few hours of frustration to get them organised on the water. Normally, teaching kayaking to westerners or Nepali boys, I would start the day by first crossing over to the other side of the lake, where the water is nice and clean – and then doing to teaching there – but I couldn't take the risk of crossing as the girls had a hard time learning to manoeuvre the kayaks. So I had to make them do the compulsory flip in the dirty water. This is always a bit of a critical state teaching anyone, flipping a kayak by purpose is often psychologically quite challenging even for people used to water sports. But this was probably the most rewarding part of the day. All the girls enjoyed flipping over the kayak and getting used to the new experience of floating in their life jackets. From here my frustration was gone. From this on, they were much more comfortable in their kayaks, and also learned to control their boats with huge smiles on their faces.

It was an enthusiastic beginning but what I learnt as the project took off was that it was going to be a lot harder than I originally thought – the reason – women's reluctance to write about themselves. I was somewhat surprised how difficult women found putting themselves at the forefront. "Oh, I don't do anything interesting. I just live my life," was a constant response; hence the chapter 'Just Living My Life'. The other thing I learned was just what busy lives we all lead. "What a fantastic idea, yes I'll do one" was often the furthest it got. To get the one hundred women I must have had contact with at least triple that number. The 'deadlines' were extended again and again.

There were often times when I nearly gave up. Family circumstances were particularly challenging during this period but always there was something to spur the project on – such as watching a documentary on the 'trafficking' of women and children in Nepal – some 15,000 per year – that's more than every man, woman and child in the town where I live, and that's a staggering 165,000 in this millennium, so far!

The philosophy behind this project is to raise funds to help women in Nepal to help themselves. By educating and empowering Nepalese women the plight of thousands of children can also be changed. Women will have real choices thereby reducing the need for early marriage and of being sold into domestic slavery or the sex industry. They will not have to work as 'beasts of burden' on the land as thousands literally do. They will not have to, heartbreakingly, give up or abandon their children because of lack of income when they become widows. They will not have to sit by the riverside all day breaking large boulders down to small stones to fill a massive basket which they then carry on their backs for a great distance to the yard, to earn just a few rupees. With 'a business' such as owning goats to sell the milk, having a mushroom farm, or their own handloom for weaving, or, more radically, learning leisure, craft, business or I.T. skills, women can support themselves, and their children, on their own earned incomes. They can also learn to work together for mutual support. Through such simple measures many, many thousands of lives can be changed and the orphanages would not be so full.

Women of the World we ask you to help us do this. We know we cannot do everything, but we can do this. Be part of this project, buy the book, spread the word and know you definitely are making a positive difference to the lives of many women and their children.

Rosa Matheson

The first projects we have chosen to assist with
the BOOK PROJECT

Himalayan Adventure Girls

Himalayan Adventure Girls is a non-profit organisation with the unique purpose of encouraging young Nepale women to participate in the outdoors industry as guides and instructors. Tourism has become one of the most important forms of income generation in Nepal and yet women in general continue to play little part. Since its founding in 2008 Himalyan Adventure Girls has sought to provide professional training and to create opportunities for Nepale women to gain meaningful employment in the outdoors industry. Until Inka and her girls created Himalayan Adventure Girls, 100% of the Nepale river guides and instructors were male. This project provides a much needed opportunity for women to gain employment as guides as well.

Today, through Himalayan Adventure Girls several young Nepale women have gained the necessary skills and experience to work as professional guides. Many have even competed in whitewater kayaking competitions, the first Nepale women to ever do so! However, as women they continue to have limited opportunities in Nepal and while they seek to continue their training it is the organisation's goal to provide new opportunities and to make sure new girls get encouragement and training.

For most women in Nepal the expectation is that they will get married young and spend the rest of their married lives at home looking after their families, a job as a guide in the rafting or trekking industry is a good opportunity for an amazing change in their lives, perhaps a way out of misery, poverty or worse. Whatever their background, the idea of this project is to empower Nepale women to work with tourists (especially female tourists). Ultimately we would like to see Nepale women travelling the world: kayaking, raft guiding, competing in international kayaking events, and using their newly acquired professional skills.

Maiti Nepal

Maiti has no literal translation but it denotes a girl's real family, the family she was born into. The word has an emotional value especially for a married Nepale woman who no longer has any rights towards her parents or their property on marrying. She then becomes an outsider belonging solely to her husband forever. The famous song, Maiti ghar timro haina paryi ghar jao – meaning "this is not your home, you belong to an outsider (husband)" says it all.

Maiti Nepal has become a home to women and girls – whether married or not – who have been exploited, neglected or their rights grossly violated by family and society. It was a crusade to find such victims a home for their safety and protection that gave birth to this NGO in November 1993 and led to the on-going fight against all the social evils inflicted on women.

Maiti Nepal was born out of a crusade to protect Nepale girls and women from crimes like domestic violence, trafficking for sex trade, child prostitution, child labour and other forms of exploitation. Most of all, its special focus has always been on preventing trafficking for forced prostitution, rescuing such victims and rehabilitating them. It also actively works to find justice for the victimized girls and women by engaging in criminal investigation and waging legal battles against the criminals.

Maiti Nepal works to help victimized Nepale girls and women regain their dignity and self-respect by providing them with an education, counselling and teaching them income generating skills.

Rotary Club of the Himalayan Gurkhas Micro-finance Project

In a truly poor village, in the district of Lamjung, live a community who depend on farming. Most of them live in dire poverty. This area has been chosen to receive micro-finance support from the Rotary Club of the Himalyan Gurkhas as part of their new 'seed-fund' project. The RC will provide a small amount of money (roughly 7,000 NRs, approximately £60), to each member, on a one year loan with small interest – 12% (this to cover the travel/food expenses of the visiting volunteer leader).

This financial help will be offered only to women in the village who live on a hand-to -mouth basis. The village community itself will select not more than ten members for each micro-credit group on the grounds that they are the most reliable and also the poorest women. With the micro-finance support, the women will be provided with livestock (pigs and/or goats), materials for small retail shops or tools and dry seeds for kitchen gardens.

A volunteer female leader will be designated as the group leader of four-to-five groups. These groups will hold their meetings at the village centre every month on the same day. The group leader will render help and training not only in the finance/credit operation but also on health and hygiene matters, thereby increasing the benefits to members.

The volunteer leader will visit the village regularly to monitor progress made by members, check all the saving books, check if animals are getting ill and offer any necessary veterinary services at the nearest location. When livestock are ready for sale the Rotary Club of the Himalyan Gurkhas will volunteer to supervise the sales of these animals at a centre with banners displayed and press coverage.

To encourage and support the poorest members of this region, RC of the Himalyan Gurkhas, after recovering the loan from this village over a period of one year, will then use the same amount for another village in the same district and gradually expand the project to other villages in other districts This project can be a long term one to cover the poorest areas of all Nepal for years to come.

the BOOK PROJECT

www.the100womenbookproject.com